21 Days of Fasting and Prayer to Reboot Your Entire Being

THE DANIEL WAY

Mac E. Whitfield Jr.

TRAINING GROUND
PUBLICATIONS

CONTENTS

DEDICATION

To the attendees of
South Post Chapel Gospel Service
USAG Yongsan, Seoul, South Korea
July 2018 – June 2019

I am truly thankful that God has destined for our lives to cross paths. My prayer is for God to reveal to each one of you that our meeting was no accident. You all were carefully handpicked by God and placed before my wife and I for us to serve you all in such a dynamic way! Thank you all for believing in the God that is within us and supporting the ministry. Without you, our assignment in this season would have never come to pass. God chose you all to be a part of our calling and for that... I am eternally grateful. I love you all with the love of Christ and dedicate this book to you.

ACKNOWLEDGEMENTS

Proverbs 3:6 says, "In all your ways acknowledge Him, and He shall direct your paths." (NKJV) I acknowledge and honor the Lord for giving me the gifts and talents to uplift God's people. Lord, thank you for gracing me with this opportunity to teach your Word in this capacity. You have created time and space for me to be obedient to your direction in writing this book. I don't claim to be an author, but I took a leap of faith while trusting you and you have proven to me that my paths are directed. Thank you for keeping your Word, despite my own insecurities. I love you Abba!

SPECIAL ACKNOWLEDGEMENTS

Colonel Monica Washington
Garrison Commander of USAG-Yongsan

Lieutenant Colonel Sang Joon "Tim" Won
Garrison Chaplain of USAG-Yongsan

Major Terry Cobban
Deputy Garrison Chaplain of USAG-Yongsan, Religious Services Office

Simply saying thank you will never match the gratitude that is planted deeply within my heart. I find it amazing to think that God can put people in your life to ensure that His Word would not go back to Him as void or invalid. You three have supported my wife and I and gave us an opportunity to exercise the gifts and callings that God has given us. As leaders and decision makers, I pray you realize that God used you to fulfill the promises of God that were spoken over our lives. As earthly vessels who are in tune with the Spirit of God, thank you for your approval in us serving as the Distinctive Religious Group Leaders of the South Post Chapel Gospel Service. It is a blessing to be able to serve the U.S. Military/Retirees, civilians, their families, and the community. If it wasn't for you all, we would not be here. Thank you so much. My wife and I salute you in the name of our Lord and Savior Jesus Christ.

HOW TO USE THIS BOOK

The Daniel Way: 21 Days of Fasting and Prayer to Reboot Your Entire Being was written as a guide for Christians who may be new to fasting, not been successful at fasting, or need some motivation while fasting. This book is unique compared to other fasting books because everything you need to know about fasting is taught in this book. It's designed to educate and keep you motivated throughout 21 full days of fasting and prayer. Additionally, there is a unique spin to the contents of the book. It includes devotionals, scripture references, prayers, and applications which involves journaling so that you can record your fasting experience and personal reflections. It even has various word puzzles that corresponds to the fasting topic for that day. This is to ensure that you remain focused on the topic at hand, meditate on God's Word, and have a little fun while growing spiritually. Each day follows this format.

Do you have to fast according to the topic for that day? Absolutely not! If you have a topic that you want to focus on for that day, then please feel free to cater the fast according to your spiritual needs. However, I ask that you stay true to the format because it is designed for every reader to be actively engaged and it helps you to grow in the areas that need God's power!

All you have to do is have faith, read, and apply. Maybe you can sit back and enjoy your time with God while drinking one of the delicious smoothies listed in this book. What? Did I forget to mention the chapter that has a variety of Daniel-friendly recipes? All you need is here! I am praying for your successful time of fasting and abstaining.

AUTHOR'S NOTE

Disclaimer: I have strived to be as accurate and complete as possible in the creation of this book, notwithstanding the fact that I am not a licensed medical provider. While all attempts have been made to verify information provided in this publication, I assume no responsibility for any or all health concerns affected by the reader while applying subject matter herein. In practical advice books, like anything else in life, there are no guarantees of desired outcome. Readers are cautioned to rely on their own judgment about their individual circumstances and to act accordingly.

This book is not intended for use as a source of healing from any ailments though it is surely possible through faith. All readers who are on medication or pregnant should continue any type of medication or dietary lifestyle that your physician has prescribed to you. If the doctor has given you specific instruction for your dietary lifestyle, please follow all instructions from your provider. I highly suggest that you talk with your physician to get an approval before starting this fast. For this reason, you may customize the fast to comply with your doctor's orders.

Chapter One

What is a fast?

Any time I do an in-depth study or may want to know the origin of a word, I always use *The New Strong's Exhaustive Concordance of the Bible.* It is an awesome resource that defines words that are written in Hebrew (Old Testament) and Greek (New Testament). It is amazing because it can reveal more revelation to the Word of God that would normally be overlooked. As I began to study the subject of fasting, I found that fasting comes from the Hebrew word **tsuwm**, (pronounced *tsoom*) which means to cover the mouth. When using this resource properly, you'll notice the "x" symbol which gives you an indication that the word is multiplied to a higher degree. For example, if we were searching for the word **blessed** followed by an "x", then you can conclude the meaning of the word would be *abundantly blessed.* In the case for the word tsuwm, the "x" symbol means *at all.* Thus, we can conclude that when you fast, you are not eating at all – absolutely nothing. So, I raise a question. If fasting means that we are not to eat anything, then why do some people utilize "The Daniel Fast" as their preferred method of fasting? Before I get into that, let's look at the meaning of fasting in the Greek. The Greek word for fasting comes from the word **nesteia** (pronounced *nace-ti-ah*) which means abstinence (from lack of food, voluntarily or religiously) So far, we can see that the Hebrew and Greek words agree that fasting means to abstain from food. But this raises another question. What about drinks?

I searched for the word fast in a Bible dictionary. It means to abstain from physical nourishment. So that eliminated every food choice and almost every kind of drink I could think of including carbonated drinks, juice, milk, coffee, tea, alcohol, and wine. But what about water? Does pure water classify as a physical nourishment? Well, yes and no. Let's briefly explore the yes-factor. Water is uniquely designed by God to be used a necessary nutrient because it is needed in volumes that exceed the body's capability to supply it. All organic chemistry reactions occur in water. It fills the area in and between cells and helps shape structures of big molecules together with protein and glycogen. Water is likewise required for digestion, absorption, transportation, dissolving nutrients, elimination of waste products and to regulate body temperature. In other words, your body needs food and water to survive, but your body can survive with water much longer than it can without food. Consider this main fact. Your body is made up of water, not food. Now let's quickly examine the no-factor. Water does not have any calories, fat, protein, nor carbohydrates. Your body loses fluid daily by breathing, sweating, and in the process of urination and excrement. Think of drinking water as a form of replenishing those liquids. Water is simply necessary to supply the need for your body to function. We are not trying to physically die here, okay? I understand that we love the Lord with all our hearts. But I'm sure that most Christians are not ready to see Him just yet. So please use godly wisdom and drink water while fasting.

From a medical standpoint, it is appropriate to fast for medical reasons. Whether its purpose is to resolve or reduce gestational health concerns, seek accurate tests, or perhaps a requirement prior to surgery, fasting under a doctor's supervision should always be followed exactly as ordered. I've seen patients who had to reschedule their surgery because they ate on surgery day when they were supposed to be fasting. In like manner, I've seen patients having to wait hours later than their scheduled surgery time only because they broke their fast by having a cup of herbal tea. Generally, these types of fasts are for 10 – 12 hours. More than likely, doctors will allow you to have small amounts of water while on the fast. Fasting times can be shorter or longer. In fact, your body is either fasting or it's not. Many people don't realize that they fast daily. Any time of the day in which you are not eating, your body is fasting. For example, the time frame from after breakfast and just before lunch, you are fasting. If you snack in between, then your body is fasting between breakfast and snack. Again, if there is any time that you are not eating, then you are fasting, especially at night during sleep. Therefore, the first meal of the day is called breakfast. You **break** your **fast** from the night before. Now that we have a clear understanding of what fasting is (both naturally and medically), let us look at some of the ideologies concerning a fast.

WHAT FASTING IS NOT

When God allows me to teach, I often share how I was raised in the church and compare it to how God raised me in the Word. I was raised in the Holiness denomination (much like Pentecostal mixed with Apostolic) which was very strict in their teaching. I truly thank God for being raised in this environment because it taught me a lot about the power of the Holy Spirit. The focal point of their teaching was to live holy before the Lord. They were some powerful men and women of God. They were some fire baptized, Holy Ghost filled, tongue-talking believers! However, there were some teachings that were focused on the literal aspect of the Word. For example, it was frowned upon if women wore earrings, make-up, and pants. Men were not to sag their pants (understandable), but it was utterly disgraceful for a man to wear a hat inside of the church. If you think this was rigid teaching, could you imagine their teaching on fasting? When starting a fast, we were taught to anoint your head with oil. You were supposed to put three drops of healing oil on the crown of your head... first drop was in the name of the Father, second drop was in the name of the Son, the third drop was in the name of the Holy Ghost. Then you were to wash your face and put some oil on your lips so that it looks like you've been eating chicken, no eating (not even a stick of gum) and no drinking (not even water). As I grew older and began to travel, I was exposed to the teachings of fasting from a variety of denominations. It seemed like every denomination conducted their fast so differently from the other. I was introduced to the Daniel Fast, the Juice Fast, and even a Facebook Fast! During that time, I laughed at what I thought was erroneous teaching. However, as I began to be around those who were hearers and doers of this teaching, I understood that fasting was taught that way in order to introduce the concept of fasting to those who have never fasted, those who were not successful at fasting, and those who really need to eliminate bad habits from their lifestyle. For example, if someone was addicted to gaming, it would be appropriate to "fast" from it in order to rid themselves of it. This goes for any addiction for that matter including smoking, alcoholism, pills, recreational drugs, social media, pornography, overeating, etc. The purpose of those teachings was put an individual in a place of abstinence. You are to "fast" those things out of your life. Although I wouldn't necessarily call abstaining from such things a fast (since fasting means to abstain from food), but I truly believe that God will honor such abstinence. Abstaining from such things (other than food) is more of a consecration rather than a fast.

CONSECRATION

Consecration means dedication to God's service. The word was used mostly in the Old Testament in reference to officially ordaining someone as a priest or kingly position. However, in the New Testament, all believers are required to consecrate themselves. It does not matter how long you have been a Christian or how much of the Bible you have memorized. If you are a believer and follower of Christ, then consecration is for you. In fact, it is impossible for us to mature in Christ without consecrating ourselves to God. As it applies to "fasting" from Netflix, TV, social media and what have you, you are literally separating yourselves from those activities for an appointed time so that you can have more time to pray, study the Word, and worship while you are fasting. As we approach the subject of consecration in the New Testament, the Word of God gives us the best explanation.

"I beseech you therefore, brethren, by the mercies of God, that you present your bodies a living sacrifice, holy, acceptable to God, *which is* your reasonable service. And do not be conformed to this world, but be transformed by the renewing of your mind, that you may prove what *is* that good and acceptable and perfect will of God." (Romans 12:1-2, NKJV)

These verses reveal the truth of what fasting, and consecration includes – sacrifice. One thing I found in common in my exposure of various teaching about fasting is that sacrifice is key. Abstaining from social media could be a sacrifice for some people. Surely abstaining from food is a sacrifice because our bodies have been conditioned to participate in it every day. I hope you realize that when you sacrifice something to God, your flesh will always be in opposition. Here it comes again. *Warfare: Spirit vs Flesh – Exposing the internal and external forces of your life.* Could this be a book title? I'm sure that you write this book every day. This is a good thing because it gives you the opportunity to work on self-control and have a disciplined lifestyle before the Lord. Just think about it. How many rewards and great opportunities have we missed because we lived a life that is undisciplined? Have you ever gotten yourself into a situation because you were undisciplined? Yeah, me too! Thank God for His grace and mercy for giving us another chance to get it right. I encourage you to win this battle between your flesh and your spirit. Use fasting, consecration, prayer, and the Word of God as weapons to pull down every stronghold of the flesh. Crucify the desires of the flesh in Jesus' name. You are more than a conqueror and you already have the victory. Men and women of God, I encourage you to see it through till the end and watch God miraculously reward you for your dedication and obedience.

Chapter Two

Biblical Examples of Fasting

Fasting is a supernatural weapon that is indispensable and beneficial to our lives. No matter if we are fasting individually or corporately, fasting can expand our relationship and growth in God. It can reveal dimensions of God in which we couldn't recognize before. Every person that has ever changed "the sector" for God has tapped into God's unlimited power and received kingdom resources and divine strategies through fasting. Although fasting has its benefits, it should never be used to manipulate God. Most Christians, today, only fast if they want something from God. It should be noted that fasting was intended to be done so that we can have a closer walk with God. Fasting was intended to seek God's face, not His hands. The purpose of fasting is to have less of ourselves and more of Him. It seems that today's Christians have somewhat disassociated themselves with the practice of fasting. Could it be that they think it no longer applies? Or perhaps we have been conditioned to have what we want and when we want it. Either way, fasting should be a lifestyle for us. As the Word of God is our greatest reference, let's look at some Old and New Testament examples of fasting. As you read these scriptures, pay close attention to how they fasted and find their results.

OLD TESTAMENT

Moses: *"So he was there with the LORD forty days and forty nights; he neither ate bread nor drank water. And He wrote on the tablets the words of the covenant, the Ten Commandments." (Exodus 34:28, NKJV)*

Actually, Moses fasted for eighty days. Two forty-day fasts without food or water (Exodus 24:18, 34:28). You should never go over three days without food or water unless you have been prompted by the Holy Spirit. I would even recommend that you consult a church leader so that you can have an accountability partner or spiritual adviser to oversee the fast. This fast that Moses was on was for a spiritual revival for God's people who had fallen into idolatry. Thus, the Standard (The Ten Commandments) by which we live today was established through fasting and prayer.

Daniel: *"I ate no pleasant food, no meat or wine came into my mouth, nor did I anoint myself at all, till three whole weeks were fulfilled." (Daniel 10:3, NKJV)*

Daniel abstained from certain types of food. He and his company did not consume any food that was offered to idols. This food was also the King's food which was served at dinner. Because Daniel didn't want to go against his own faith, he decided to eat a diet that consisted of raw vegetables, fruits, and water (Daniel 1:12-17; 10:2,3). After Daniel and his company abstained from the King's meal, they went through great mental, spiritual, physical, and emotional warfare. So, this type of "fast" should be entered in times of spiritual warfare or when we need to seek God for wisdom and revelation. Daniel's fast loosed angels, bound demons, and brought supernatural understanding and insight into the End-Times (Daniel 10:12-14). A huge benefit from Daniel's abstinence is that the foods he ate released healing to the whole body because it put the body in a state of detoxification and purification. Unlike the fast that Jesus went on, Daniel was still able to perform difficult work.

One note of caution; you may experience headaches while detoxing.

Ezra: *"Then I proclaimed a fast there at the river of Ahava, that we might humble ourselves before our God, to seek from Him the right way for us and our little ones and all our possessions. For I was ashamed to request of the king an escort of soldiers and horsemen to help us against the enemy on the road, because we had spoken to the king, saying, 'The hand of our God is upon all those for good who seek Him, but His power and His wrath are against all those who forsake Him.' So we fasted and entreated our God for this, and He answered our prayer." (Ezra 8:21-23, NKJV)*

Ezra fasted differently from Daniel in terms of purpose. Ezra needed protection for his finances and possessions. The book of Ezra depicts the story of Ezra and his company going on a long journey back to Jerusalem from Babylon. This city is where the Jews became captive. However, they settled down in this place and became very wealthy – so wealthy that some of the Jews didn't want to go back to Jerusalem. The Jews who remained in Babylon were required to send gold and silver with Ezra so that the Temple could be rebuilt. But Ezra knew that there were thieves waiting to attack during the journey. So, Ezra decided to call a corporate fast among the chief fathers, priests, and others who were assigned to assist him in his mission. Although the Bible did not give any details on how they fasted or how long they fasted, but it includes the purpose of the corporate fast. The fast was for divine protection of his finances and possessions while in transit. Notice that Ezra didn't fast to escape the problem, but he fasted so that he could have help in solving the problem. If you are facing a major change in your life, this is the type of fast in which you should go on.

David: *"David therefore pleaded with God for the child, and David fasted and went in and lay all night on the ground." (2 Samuel 12:16, NKJV)*

Now here was man who had a heart for God, but he wasn't perfect either. King David committed adultery with Bathsheba and got the woman pregnant. Then he came up with a plan (I mean a lie) to try to pass the baby as her husband's child, but that didn't work. So, he had Bathsheba's husband killed so that the truth won't come out. Even though David repented, he still had to be punished for the sins he committed. When the baby was born, the Lord struck the baby with an illness and David fasted hoping that the Lord would give mercy and spare the child's life. The Lord did not grant David's request. When the baby died, David got up, washed and groomed himself, went into the temple and worshipped God. This tells us 2 important facts about fasting. First, fasting is a meaningful way to approach God when we are serious about the need of being in His presence. Secondly, we must understand that fasting is not a formula to manipulate the Lord. It is not a way to prepare God for our will, but rather fasting is a way for us to prepare for His will.

JONAH: "*So the people of Nineveh believed God, proclaimed a fast, and put on sackcloth, from the greatest to the least of them. Then word came to the king of Nineveh; and he arose from his throne and laid aside his robe, covered himself with sackcloth and sat in ashes. And he caused it to be proclaimed and published throughout Nineveh by the decree of the king and his nobles, saying, 'Let neither man nor beast, herd nor flock, taste anything; do not let them eat, or drink water. But let man and beast be covered with sackcloth, and cry mightily to God; yes, let every one turn from his evil way and from the violence that is in his hands. Who can tell if God will turn and relent, and turn away from His fierce anger, so that we may not perish?' Then God saw their works, that they turned from their evil way; and God relented from the disaster that He had said He would bring upon them, and He did not do it.*" (Jonah 3:5-10, NKJV)

There are times when we need to fast corporately or for repentance. In this case, it was both! As you read from the scripture, the king was so serious about the nation's fast, that he even put animals on a fast! That caught God's attention, and God lifted His judgement off them during that time.

The Old Testament has several examples of fasting. I've listed a few more if you would like to study them.

Elijah: "*So he arose, and ate and drank; and he went in the strength of that food forty days and forty nights as far as Horeb, the mountain of God.*" (1 Kings 19:8, NKJV)

Esther: "*Go, gather all the Jews who are present in Shushan, and fast for me; neither eat nor drink for three days, night or day. My maids and I will fast likewise. And so I will go to the king, which is against the law; and if I perish, I perish!*" (Ester 4:16, NKJV)

Hannah: "*So it was, year by year, when she went up to the house of the* LORD, *that she provoked her; therefore she wept and did not eat.* (1Samuel 1:7, NKJV)

NEW TESTAMENT

Paul: "*And he was three days without sight, and neither ate nor drank.*" (Acts 9:9, NKJV)

The Apostle Paul fasted after he surrendered to Christ. The Bible declared that he didn't eat nor drink for three days. No food. No water. Paul was completely changed by the power of God. His whole foundation was confronted. As you can see, this type of fast should only be done in extreme times of crisis, like Esther. Again, wisdom should be applied when on this type of fast. The most one can go without food or water is three days before your body begins to break down its vital organs. This type of fast requires desperation in the times of crisis. It will surely expand our prayer life and relationship with God while crucifying the flesh. It takes us into a state of humility, repentance, and brokenness. So please ensure that you are under the direction of the Holy Spirit before and during this type of fast.

Jesus: *"Then Jesus was led up by the Spirit into the wilderness to be tempted by the devil. 2 And when He had fasted forty days and forty nights, afterward He was hungry." (Matthew 4:1-2, NKJV)*

Another point of view from the same story.

Jesus: *"Then Jesus, being filled with the Holy Spirit, returned from the Jordan and was led by the Spirit into the wilderness, being tempted for forty days by the devil. And in those days He ate nothing, and afterward, when they had ended, He was hungry." (Luke 4:1-2, NKJV)*

Many Bible scholars and theologians believe that when Jesus fasted during this time, He only drank water. Their justification is noticing that the Bible said nothing about Him being thirsty. Another justification for their belief is determined by what Jesus was tempted by. Satan tempted Jesus to turn the stones into bread...never being tempted with water. Studies have shown that the average human body of an adult can go 50 – 60 days on water alone without harmful effects. You should apply wisdom if you are going to go on this type of fast. The body will need to be gradually conditioned to live on water alone.

John the Baptist: *"For John the Baptist came neither eating bread nor drinking wine, and you say, 'He has a demon." (Luke 7:33, NKJV)*

"Now John himself was clothed in camel's hair, with a leather belt around his waist; and his food was locusts and wild honey." (Matthew 3:4, NKJV)

In this example, John the Baptist's diet was also restricted – not eating bread or drinking wine and eating locusts and wild honey. This dietary restriction was very similar to Jesus' dietary restriction when he was young (Isaiah 7:14-15). You could consider John the Baptist's fast a partial fast, as he was still eating in general. This type of fast helped him walk in the spirit and discipline his flesh from its appetites. This kind of fast also helps to overcome addiction, flawed character, lust, etc. It is a way to bring the flesh under subjection of Christ's authority.

The New Testament speaks about fasting as well. By this time in history, fasting was culturally practiced. Below are some verses to let you know that people were fasting in the New Testament. The last verse listed here is what Jesus had to say about our character during a fast.

Cornelius: *"So Cornelius said, "Four days ago I was fasting until this hour; and at the ninth hour I prayed in my house, and behold, a man stood before me in bright clothing, and said, 'Cornelius, your prayer has been heard, and your alms are remembered in the sight of God." (Acts 10:30-31, NKJV)*

Marriage: *"Do not deprive one another except with consent for a time, that you may give yourselves to fasting and prayer; and come together again so that Satan does not tempt you because of your lack of self-control." (1 Corinthians 7:5, NKJV)*

Ministry: *"As they ministered to the Lord and fasted, the Holy Spirit said, "Now separate to Me Barnabas and Saul for the work to which I have called them." (Acts 13:2, NKJV)*

Promotion/Position/Decision-Making: *"So when they had appointed elders in every church, and prayed with fasting, they commended them to the Lord in whom they had believed. (Acts 14:23, NKJV)*

The Character of Fasting: *"Moreover, when you fast, do not be like the hypocrites, with a sad countenance. For they disfigure their faces that they may appear to men to be fasting. Assuredly, I say to you, they have their reward. But you, when you fast, anoint your head and wash your face, so that you do not appear to men to be fasting, but to your Father who is in the secret place; and your Father who sees in secret will reward you openly. (Matthew 6:16-18, NKJV)*

Chapter Three

Types of Fasts and Fasting Terms

This book is centered around the Daniel Fast, but you don't have to fast in the same manner as Daniel fasted. There are other types of fasts as well. A good reason to keep this in mind is because everyone does not have the same diet. It would be redundant for vegetarians or vegans to go on the Daniel Fast since they share a similar diet. The Daniel Fast would not be such a sacrifice for them. I would suggest for vegetarians, vegans, or those who share a similar diet like the Daniel fast to fast by skipping a meal or two. Or, you can fast by time. For example, you could fast from 6:00am – 12:00pm for beginners; 6:00am – 3:00pm for intermediates; 6:00am – 6:00pm for advanced; and 24 hours if you are well experienced with fasting. Below is a list and explanations of different types of fasts.

Absolute Fast or Dry Fast- This type of fast means to abstain from food and water. For example, Paul fasted when he was blinded by Christ. He went three days without food or water. Please be Spirit-led when attempting to go on this type of fast. A person should never go more than three days without water.

Normal Fast- This type of fast consists of abstaining from all food, not water.

Partial Fast or the Daniel Fast- Fasting partially means that you will be abstaining from certain types of foods and drinks. You can think of it as a dietary restriction or simply skipping a meal or two.

Liquid Fast- A fast that only allows you to drink liquids and abstain from all solid food. Most people will drink water and natural juices (from a juicer). Please be careful while drinking juices because they are loaded with natural sugar. There are some who would include soup or broth with no solid foods in the soup.

Corporate Fast- This type of fast explains the participants of a fast, not necessarily the application of a fast. Corporate fasts consist of a group of participants such as a church, family, leaders, a nation, etc. Usually, fasting with others consists of concerns that are agreeable for all participants.

Personal Fast- This type fast is only for you and about you. What you are fasting for (or fasting from) is only between you and God.

Media Fast- A fast from all types of media such as TV, social media, gaming, and other forms of entertainment. Most people who fast from the media are refocusing themselves to the Lord to refrain from distractions.

Lifestyle of Fasting and Prayer- This classification of fasting is not meant to focus on His provision. Amazingly, some people only fast when they want something from God. The purpose of having a lifestyle of fasting and prayer is to get closer to God, not to get anything else other than more of Him.

Chapter Four

Why Should Christians Fast?

When explaining the physical aspect of fasting, most people would wonder why they should restrict their diet, or they'll be consumed with the health benefits of fasting while never really grasping the concept of developing spiritually. Some may not understand how restricting their diet strengthens their spirit. I will attempt to explain the connection of fasting and spiritual growth and why we as Christians should have a fasting lifestyle.

The main point of fasting is to draw closer to God. It is a necessary way to cut off the physical world which wants to claim itself as the authority of your physical body in the earth. In other words, the world says, "If it wasn't for me and my system, you would not be here." Then we have the spiritual aspect of our being which says, "Your spirit is connected to God,

I allow the connection for God to use you so that He may be revealed in the earth." This, my friends, is the war that we are in everyday! For our spirit to be stronger than our flesh, we must feed our spirit more than our flesh. Therefore, we should abstain from food and earthly activities while fasting so that we can exercise our spirit man by drawing closer to God. As we draw closer to God, He begins to strengthen us and gives us tools that we need to live in the earth.

I personally think that fasting today is more challenging than fasting in the Old and New Testaments. Back then, their world was defined by power, money, and influence – much like today. Yet, on top of this, we have so many distractions. I'm sure they had their distractions as well, but they surely didn't have the modern conveniences like we have today. Electronic equipment, gadgets, and entertainment is available to us at a click of a finger at any time of the day or night. It just never goes off! When I was a little boy, I remember when TV went off the air. At midnight, the American National Anthem would play and after that, there was only static until the next day. Nowadays, TV and other forms of convenient entertainment is here to distract you any time you allow it. Through these forms of entertainment, we become conditioned to act, feel, and become a certain way. These distractions can restrict our thinking to focus on our physical needs and wants. As a result, our self-worth and self-meaning have diminished while becoming imbalanced between our material and spiritual needs. Not only do we lean towards what we want, be we have the audacity to dictate when we get what we want. We want what we want, and we want it now! We have become a microwave generation. Have you ever put some food in a microwave and set it to "cook" for 1-minute? You go back to the microwave 30 seconds later and say, "It ain't done yet?" Have you ever caught yourself doing that? Me too! We can be imbalanced to the point where we can't wait 60 seconds to get what we want.

To combat this imbalance that we can all have from time to time, we need to grow spiritually by looking inwardly instead of outwardly counting on these disposable treasures. Self-examination goes beyond recalling the things that happened throughout the day, week, or month. It is more of looking closely at your responses and reactions. You can examine your thoughts, feelings, beliefs, and motives. Ask God if those things reflect His presence and glory. Your experiences, the decisions you make, the relationships you have, and the things you engage in will give you a reflection of your relationship with Christ. Examining these aspects of your life can provide useful insights on what you may need to work on or work out of your life. It will challenge you to act, react, and conduct yourself in any given situation. There is hope in Christ. All you have to do is learn His Word and become obedient to His Word. Seek the truth of God and apply it to your life. Be loving and forgiving to yourself and others. As you fast with this in mind, the Lord will teach and equip you to handle and alter your imperfections. But you must trust Him with your whole heart.

Fasting can also develop your potentials. Remember when the disciples couldn't cast a demon out of the boy? Jesus replied, "Because of your unbelief... and this kind comes out by prayer and fasting." (Matthew

17:19-21) If you believe, and don't doubt, fasting can strengthen your courage, power, authority which will cause you to overcome obstacles. Fasting helps with overcoming addictions, self-doubt, fear, unbelief, and so much more. In the Bible, Esther was facing a challenge as well. She called a fast for her people when she was about to approach the king, something that was unlawful at the time because you had to be summoned to be in a king's presence. However, she conquered her fear and approached the king with her request. God saw fit for her request to be granted. I truly believe if she did not believe, coupled with her fasting, the story might have not ended the way it did. Sampson is another example. His diet was restricted from birth due to a vow his parents made. He was the strongest man alive during his time. Yes, he surly had weaknesses, but his strength served God for a purpose. Again, if he had not stuck to his dietary restriction, it is possible that his strength would not be used for the plan of God or allowed him to come to terms with why he was chosen to be so "different".

Some people may fast to find a meaning to their life. Jesus fasted for forty days and forty nights. Not long after that he was tempted by Satan. Though he overcame, He still had to face a hard truth – His life's purpose. Although He was tempted to not fulfill His mission, He surrendered to God's plan. Fasting was a way for Him to gain perspective of His reason to live and His reason to die. We are so different in our perception. We sometimes forcefully give meaning to our lives because we think that our life's meaning is self-directed instead of God-determined. Fasting helps you realize that we are nothing without God. We cannot exist without Him.

I am simply saying that fasting is a way to show God that He is in control of it all. When you do that, He will show you your life's meaning, and we don't have to pollute it with our idea of life's meaning. Fast, and search for your meaning.

You can also fast for others. Sometimes you may be led to fast and pray for others to receive salvation or overcome life's challenges. You may be led by God to fast for someone's marriage or deliverance. It is such an honor to humbly sacrifice an aspect of your life so that others can come into the knowledge of God's truth. Remember, Esther was not only fasting for herself, but also for her people.

There are many examples in the Bible that shows us why we should fast. Fasting can be a spiritual weapon in times of warfare as well as an "upgrade" for our prayers. It can also cleanse our body and soul. In fact, studies show that fasting decreases many diseases that are common to our culture such as cancer, diabetes, and heart related issues.

In any case, Jesus expects us to have a lifestyle of prayer and fasting. Jesus says in Matthew, chapter 6, "When you give.... When you pray... and ... When you fast." Although this may sound foundational, it is so important to our committed life and faith. It is an act of humility before God that we might have power to serve our Lord and to accomplish all that He has intended for us that Christ may be glorified on earth.

Chapter Five

When Should Christians Fast?

The only time fasting and prayer was required was during the Day of Atonement, which was in the Old Testament law. It was custom to fast and pray to be reconciled with God. This fast was attached to repentance. *See* Jeremiah 36:6. Moses fasted for 40 days and 40 nights to seek the Lord. His fast was attached to needing a Word for his people. *See* Exodus 34:28. King Jehoshaphat called a corporate fast because he and his people were about to be attacked. His fast was attached to protection and warfare. *See* 2 Chronicles 20:3. The entire city of Nineveh including their animals fasted. Their fast was attached to repentance and mercy from God's judgement. *See* Jonah 3:5. David fasted when he found out that his king and best friend (Saul and Jonathan) had been killed. His fast was attached to mourning. *See* 2 Samuel 1:12. Nehemiah fasted when he found out that Jerusalem was still in ruins. His fast was attached to God's provision. *See* Nehemiah 1:4.

You see, there is not a set time in which you are to pray and fast. Fasting is not a ritual. So, you can fast and pray anytime you want. However, from the examples I stated above, we can gather evidence that prayer and fasting was done during times of trouble or distress. If we have a lifestyle of fasting and prayer, then we would not have to wait until something "bad" happens to get into the mindset of fasting and prayer. I believe that we can have fasts and prayers stored in heaven so that when trouble comes, you are not shaken by its stress. Fasting and prayer can also increase your faith and your relationship with God.

What time of the day should we fast? Now that's an interesting question. In the Old Testament, people who were fasting did not work. They spent their day praying and fasting. It's more difficult to do that today because we must work. However, you can still be successful at fasting even if you are busy at work. During work hours, you can continue to abstain from the thing you are fasting from. During lunch break, you could go to a quiet place and read the Word of God and pray before you return to duty. When you get home, you can further apply the spiritual aspect of fasting which includes prayer, studying the Word, praise, worship, and meditation. However, if work allows little room for you to focus on God, then consider fasting when you get home until it's time to go back to work the next day. Can you think of other ways to revise your schedule so that you can have quality time with God?

Chapter Six

How to Start and End a Fast

When it comes to the physical portion of a fast, preparing for a successful fast is very important; so please make sure that you plan ahead! A great way to do this is to write your menu and shopping list before you start your fast. Below are a few tips to help you get started.

1. Start the fast by focusing on your faith.

Many people focus on the physical side of fasting and tend to neglect the spiritual side. Whichever fast you decide to go on, ensure that you focus on your faith. Fasting includes your entire mind, body and spirit. Pray and ask God for guidance, strength, and authority to deny self and battle physical cravings. These physical cravings are not just food. It could be from other forms of addiction or carnal things that distracts us from fellowship with God.

2. Eat lighter as you approach the first day of your fast.

In my experience, it's always a good idea to slowly transition into a fast. I highly suggest the same for you as well. Caffeine from coffee, tea, and sodas can be just as addictive as smoking and drinking alcohol. So, you would want to gradually ween yourself from it. I know it is tempting to eat your favorite meal and in large quantity before you start your fast. This can create significant challenges in the first days of the fast. This is not your "Last Supper"! Use wisdom.

3. Be prepared for withdrawal symptoms.

On the Daniel Fast as well as many food-restricted fasts, removing processed food filled with chemicals may cause withdrawal symptoms like fatigue, headaches, or muscle cramps. To prevent or reduce these symptoms, make sure you drink enough water; at least eight glasses per day. I can't express this enough. Your body needs water. So, drink, drink, drink!

4. Keep a high energy level.

Protein-rich foods such as beans and nuts will help you to keep your energy level high. It is recommended that adult men need 56 grams of protein per day and adult women need about 46 grams of protein per day. Oranges, lemons, and other forms of Vitamin C can help with your energy levels and it helps to detoxify your body.

5. Stock your kitchen

Particularly with The Daniel Fast, your food choices become limited. Before you start your fast, make sure that you have plenty of fruits and vegetables. This fast would be difficult to continue if you were to run out of the foods you can eat. So, make sure there is plenty (if you can) for breakfast, lunch, dinner, and snacks.

6. Plan, plan, plan.

If you are planner, then it may be helpful to record your daily meals in advance. This can help you avoid the temptation of breaking the fast. Think of it as writing a clear vision of your goal. Read it and stick with it.

7. Don't give up.

If you mistakenly eat something that you shouldn't during the fast, it is better to ask for forgiveness and continue than to completely stop the fast. Ask God to help you remember your restrictions. Have faith in Him to give you power to refrain from making that mistake again. Giving up is what the enemy wants you to do. Consider your salvation as an example. If you sin after you received salvation, would you just say forget it and turn your back on God? No! You would repent, ask for forgiveness, and pray so that you can become stronger in your weakness. You must do the same when you are fasting. Do not give up!

HOW TO END THE FAST

Similar to how we prepared ourselves to go on a fast, we should also end the fast just as carefully. A slow decrease of foods when you start your fast, and a slow increase of foods when you end. Years ago, when I was on the Daniel Fast, I had jumped right into my favorite meal with no gradual increase of foods. On the last day of my fast, at 11:58 pm, I found myself in line at McDonalds. As soon as the clock read 12:01 am, the lady behind the counter said, "Hello sir, may I take your order?" I replied, "Yes ma'am, let me get numbers 1 through 5!" Not all the food was for me, but my mind was set on getting 21 days' worth of meat. I tell you the truth, I shocked my body in such a way that it caused me so much irritation in my digestive system. I learned a fast lesson for that season. I would not want you to have to go through the same thing. However, you know your body better than I do. So, please use wisdom during your transition into and out of a fast. You never know, you may learn a thing or two that you may want to incorporate into your diet for the rest of your life.

As for the spiritual side of ending your fast, have faith that the issues you brought before the Lord are settled in heaven. Continue to serve God while you wait for the manifestations of His promises. Accept His answers to your prayers even if His answer is, "No." Understand that God knows all and has invested so much into your life. He knows what is best for you. As you sign back into your Netflix or social media accounts, return to eating meat, or whatever you had abstained from, continue to exercise self-control. Do not let these things control you.

Chapter Seven

Spend Time with God While Fasting

I understand that you are busy most days. Many of you have full-time jobs and careers. You are slammed with preparing for the next meeting and it seems as if work never stops. Even if you do have a free weekend, you could be called into work or it becomes filled with other people's agenda. Some of you may volunteer. Well that's another job of itself especially if you are a part of an organization that doesn't have many volunteers. This would mean that your work load increases. Many of you have the responsibilities of a husband or wife. You must set time aside for them to ensure they are not neglected. Many of you have the responsibilities of being a parent. Your children need you according to the stage of life that they're in. Your friend may call you up and ask for some advice or just to talk about what they are going through. So, you set time aside for them, and before you know it, it's time to wake up and do it all over again. So, you find yourself having no time for yourself and no time for God. So many things could be going on at the same time and may cause you to become imbalanced. Does this sound like you?

Without God, my life would be horribly imbalanced. I juggle so much during the day that sometimes I am surprised that God has graced me to do it. However, I'm not perfect either. I still find myself being challenged with time. One thing I found out is that I cannot put God on the backburner at the end of my day. He must come first because it is Him who gives me strength from day-to-day. If you find yourself in a similar situation, then I suggest that you spend some time with God through prayer, reading/studying the Bible, and in worship.

Prayer is a powerful weapon all by itself, but when it is coupled with fasting, it intensifies. You can pray without fasting, but you can't fast without praying. It goes together. Without prayer, your fasting will be done in vain and it will not be effective to your spiritual growth. Prayer and fasting need one another. Just like the Bible says that without faith, it is impossible to please God (Hebrew 11:6), so is fasting without prayer is nothing more than a diet. When prayer and fasting are one, it can accelerate the breakthrough that you desire. We become less so that He becomes more. You see, prayer is about power and miracles. It's about planting and uprooting. It's about laboring and breakthroughs. It's about establishing or legislating. Most of all, prayer is about communication with the Father. It amazes me how so many people want God to do this and that for them, but they don't like to communicate with Him.

Sometimes I think that maybe they just don't know how to pray. Then I think, well maybe they don't want to know how to pray. Consider this; if you loved someone and you desired to talk to them, then wouldn't you put forth the effort to communicate with him or her? If you were deaf, would you try to find a means to communicate with that person even if you had to go through a learning curve to achieve that result? We should have the same mentality when it comes to communicating with God. Prayer is the direct connection that is used to communicate with the Father. The other part of prayer is listening to God. Some people do pray, but don't take the time to listen. It is as if they go to God with a wish list like He's some kind of genie in a bottle. Prayer does not work that way. Sometimes we need to get into the presence of God and just listen. He might speak to you. Let the peace of God within you be the judge.

Reading and studying the Word of God is a sure way to spend time with Him. In times of fasting, reading scriptures concerning the reason why you are fasting will help you find the answer for what you are seeking God for. Spending time with God will allow you to become open to His Spirit and receive revelations. If God tells you something, He will always back it up in His Word. What you hear in your spirit should not be different from what is written in the Bible. Therefore, you can learn to know when God is speaking to you.

Praising and worshiping God is another way that you can spend time with Him. The Lord loves to be adored. He loves when you can call on His name. It catches His attention. Your praise is telling God that you are recognizing that He is worthy of your notice. Praising God tells God that you approve of Him. Your praise confirms who He is. It can be privately or publicly, but most of all, it should stem from your heart. In return, He lives in your praise and causes you to become blessed. When you worship Him, it causes Him to arise! When you worship Him, it causes Him to draw near to you. When you worship Him, you become the place where He dwells. Praise God for His Word that says He inhabits the praises of His people! Let God arise in your praise and worship as you fast and may all your enemies (naturally and spiritually) be scattered!

Chapter Eight

The Benefits of Fasting

I know that fasting is not something that everybody enjoys. It is a sacrifice. In my experience, people do not like to be inconvenienced – even more of a reason to go on a fast. You must change your mindset when it comes to fasting. If you have a negative perception towards fasting, then you'll never understand its benefits. Fasting can benefit your mind, body, and spirit. Let's examine this a bit further.

Many people report that fasting allowed them to have a clear mind. Usually, this happens to me when my body has fully adjusted to the fast. I found that I can understand concepts easier and make sound decisions. My mental stress can diminish substantially, and I feel as though I can think with clarity. It's important to have a sound mind and have control over your thoughts because everything that comes to your mind is not from God. Therefore, the Bible proclaims, "Casting down imaginations, and every high thing that exalts itself against the knowledge of God and bringing into captivity every thought to the obedience of Christ." (2 Corinthians 10:5, KJV) These thoughts will come, and fasting will give you strength to overcome any mental instability. You will have the authority to combat the lies or false confirmations and apply the truth of God (scriptures) that says the opposite. For example, you may notice that you have been coughing regularly. The enemy may bring a spirit of fear upon you and tell you that it is cancer. You have the responsibility to say no to that negative thought and say, "By Jesus' stripes, I am healed!" You can overcome thoughts of failure, suicide, guilt, unsuccessfulness, and blame. Fasting gives you the strength to stand against the enemy while using the Word of God as your backbone! Perhaps you may have an addiction to gaming. Fasting can ween you off the desire to be mentally stimulated. Technology is ruling the world. So many people are using these virtual realities to escape real life responsibilities. Fasting can help you have a healthy and balanced life.

Fasting significantly benefits your body. If you approach your fast as Daniel did or perhaps a juice fast, you will put your body in a state of detoxing. With so many processed foods we have today, detoxing is a great way to stay healthy especially if you do it naturally with certain types of organic foods. Studies have shown that fasting can also prevent or reduce ailments such as diabetes, heart conditions, and cancer. If you stick to the fast, you'll notice that your body will start to change. So, don't be surprised if you notice that you've lost weight, see changes in your excrement, or even changes in your skin. It has been reported that some people noticed that their skin became smoother while fasting. The Bible records that after Daniel abstained from the king's meat, he was fair to look upon and he was fatter (not in terms of weight gain, but in terms of being healthier and stronger). *See* Daniel 1:15. I've also found that my energy levels tremendously increased days into the fast. I am more enthusiastic about taking on tasks or completing them. High levels of energy coupled with a clear mind can make significant changes in your life. Please keep in mind that every physical body responds differently. You know your body better than anybody else!

Your spirit man can also benefit from fasting. By abstaining from food or certain foods to tame your flesh, fasting gives you an opportunity to exercise your spirit, building it in the ways of the Lord. Just as the body needs exercise, your spirit does as well. Fasting teaches your spirit to become subject to the Holy Spirit. You allow God room to shift around some things in your life.

As it pertains to shifting some things around in your life, think of it as a welcoming. When you invite someone into your home, it is custom to ensure that they feel comfortable and welcomed. A good host or hostess would ask them to have a seat. You would offer them something to drink or maybe you have prepared some snacks. You might ask if the temperature is okay for them. Now if that same guest would come into your home and put their feet on your table, rearrange your furniture, and take pictures down from your walls, you would say that is disrespectful, right? When you invite Christ into your life to be your Lord and Savior, He has a way of disrespecting the strongholds and mindsets that you've established. Therefore, He's no longer a visitor but the owner of your "home". *"The earth is the Lord's, and the fulness thereof; the world, and they that dwell therein." (Psalms 24:1, KJV)* It takes humility to allow God to change and rearrange things in your life. Fasting gives you the strength to humble yourself and allow those changes to take place. You can become more disciplined and discipled by God if you allow Christ to be Lord over every area of your life. Fasting can be a tool used to activate your humility while God continues to transform your life into the image of Christ.

Chapter Nine

The Symptoms of Fasting

Just as there are benefits to fasting, there are also symptoms of fasting. If you don't enjoy fasting, then I'm sure you won't enjoy some of its possible symptoms. You want to talk about a sacrifice? In my years of fasting, I've seen people break their fast, not because they didn't want to do it, but because they could not handle the symptoms of fasting. The symptoms they had experienced inconvenienced them. I've already told you that people don't like to be inconvenienced. So, they decided not to push forward with their fast. Circling back to the mindset of fasting. You must stay positive and keep your faith that God is pleased with your fast. I encourage you not to give up but press towards the mark. The symptoms of fasting can also affect your mind, body, and spirit. I will attempt to expose some symptoms that you may experience during your season of fasting.

Most symptoms of fasting will begin in the first few days or week of fasting. Those symptoms can affect you mentally. Do you remember the old saying, "Things will get worse before it gets better"? Well, that is the general idea. When you start to fast, you may quickly become discouraged. Just as those negative thoughts come in, you may be tempted to break your fast or simply quit. The stresses of life do not stop just because you are fasting. On the contrary, it may intensify. Your mind must process what your body and spirit is going through. Think of it as a ball of yarn or wires. You would normally have all these things balled up in your thought life as if your mind is thinking about several things at once. When you start fasting, your mind begins to unravel or detangle. It starts to set things in order. If you are not used to thinking this way, this could affect your judgement until it becomes settled. Your temptations can increase as well. Just think about it. You may be at work and its lunch time. All your co-workers are eating a big juicy burger, and you're eating vegetables. Maybe you are cooking dinner for your children that consists of all the food you may be abstaining from. Not only do you have to cook it and smell it, but you also watch them eat it. That can be a great temptation for some. Especially if you are used to tasting the food while you are cooking it.

You will definitely see symptoms in your body while fasting. We already discussed the possibility of you losing weight and having clearer or smoother skin. However, it has been reported that some people will have outbreaks before their skin clears. This symptom is manifested because your body is detoxing, and all the oils and toxins are coming out of your skin. Your digestive system can also change. You may find that your bowel movements are regular, or you may become gassy. Your breath may become unfriendly. You may have stronger headaches and hunger pangs. You may experience dizziness or nausea. The list goes on. Jesus taught that we shouldn't appear to be fasting as if we are gloomy and in distress. He taught us to appear as we normally do. So, as it pertains to your body, make sure that you continue to practice good hygiene.

When it comes to your spirit-man, you'll see symptoms in the spirit as well although you may not notice it at first. When you begin to fast and pray, it is like setting off an alarm in the spiritual realm. The Kingdom of God knows that you are fasting, and the kingdom of darkness knows that you are fasting as well. The last thing the enemy wants you to do is to get closer to God. So, he will use anything he can to distract you from your prayers and fast. He knows that when you decide to seek God for your life, you are one step closer to your destiny. The Bible says, "For the LORD God *is* a sun and shield; The LORD will give grace and glory; no good *thing* will He withhold from those who walk uprightly." (Psalm 84:11, NKJV) If you are walking in the ways of the Lord, the enemy knows that you will get the next piece of your puzzle if you start to fast and pray. He wants to stop you from receiving another piece of your puzzle. This is one symptom (or sign) to let you know that you are headed in the right direction. It's time for warfare! The Lord will protect you in battle. You have the victory! So, don't give up!

The Daniel Way Food List

In general, foods that are allowed on the Daniel Fast consists of vegetables, fruits, legumes, whole grains, nuts, and water. These foods can be fresh, canned or dried. However, please be mindful of canned foods because oftentimes canned foods have a lot of preservatives and other chemicals in them. PLEASE READ THE LABELS!!! Avoid sugar at all cost. There are many different names for sugar in which some are listed below. Watch out for these ingredients.

barley malt, cane sugar, corn syrup, dextrose, fructose, glucose, high-fructose, corn syrup, maltodextrin, sucrose.

Also avoid chemicals, artificial preservatives, and other additives as much as possible. Rule of thumb: If you don't recognize it as a food, avoid it!

Bread is allowed only if it is whole wheat and unleavened (no yeast). Some people would allow 100% raw honey. Please allow the Holy Spirit to guide you on how to customize the fast accordingly. Listed below are the types of foods that are allowed in *The Daniel Way*.

FOODS THAT ARE ALLOWED
(fresh, canned, or dried)

All fruits. fresh, frozen, dried, juiced or canned. Fruits include but are not limited to apples, apricots, bananas, blackberries, blueberries, boysenberries, cantaloupe, cherries, cranberries, figs, grapefruit, grapes, guava, honeydew melon, kiwi, lemons, limes, mangoes, nectarines, oranges, papayas, peaches, pears, pineapples, plums, prunes, raisins, raspberries, strawberries, tangelos, tangerines, watermelon etc.

All vegetables. These can be fresh, frozen, dried, juiced or canned. Vegetables include but are not limited to artichokes, asparagus, beets, broccoli, Brussels sprouts, cabbage, carrots, cauliflower, celery, chili peppers, collard greens, corn, cucumbers, eggplant, garlic, ginger root, kale, leeks, lettuce, mushrooms, mustard greens, okra, onions, parsley, potatoes, radishes, rutabagas, scallions, spinach, sprouts, squashes, sweet potatoes, tomatoes, turnips, watercress, yams, zucchini, veggie burgers are an option if you are not allergic to soy.

All whole grains, including but not limited to whole wheat, brown rice, millet, quinoa, oats, barley, grits, whole wheat pasta, whole wheat tortillas, rice cakes and popcorn.

All nuts and seeds, including but not limited to sunflower seeds, cashews, peanuts, sesame. Natural peanut butter is okay as well.

All legumes. These can be canned or dried. Legumes include but are not limited to dried beans, pinto beans, split peas, lentils, black eyed peas, kidney beans, black beans, cannellini beans, white beans.

Other: tofu, soy products, vinegar, seasonings, salt, herbs and spices.

FOODS THAT ARE NOT ALLOWED

All meat to include animal products, fish and other seafood – nothing from an animal; All dairy products; All artificial sweeteners; Sodas, Coffee, Tea; Energy Drinks; Alcohol and Wine.

Recipes

Overnight Coconut Oatmeal
Servings: 4

Ingredients
2 cups rolled oats
1 cup canned coconut milk
Toppings: shredded coconut, berries, bananas, granola, chopped nuts

Directions
In a medium size bowl mix the rolled oats and coconut milk with 1 cup of water. Divide the overnight coconut oatmeal between 4 1-cup mason jars or small bowls. Cover and leave in your fridge overnight. In the morning, enjoy the oatmeal cold with any or all the toppings.

Notes
Turn this recipe into a single serving breakfast by using ½ cup oats, ¼ cup coconut milk and ¼ cup of water. The overnight oats are best eaten within 12 hours but will last up to 4 days in your fridge.

Overnight Banana Cinnamon Crock Pot Oatmeal
Prep Time: 5 min   Cook time: 8 hours   Servings: 4

Ingredients
2 cups old-fashioned oats (not the quick cook kind): 2 cups
3½ cups water

2 cups almond or coconut milk
1 Tablespoon cinnamon
2 bananas, mashed
1 banana, sliced for garnish (optional)

Directions
Using non-stick cooking spray, thoroughly spray the bottom and sides of the Crock Pot insert. Add the old-fashioned oats, water, milk, and cinnamon to the crock pot. Mix well until all ingredients are well incorporated. Cover and cook on the low setting for 8 hours. Prior to serving, stir in the mashed bananas. Garnish with additional banana slices if desired.

Apricot Walnut Energy Bars
Prep Time: 15 min

Ingredients
1 cup walnuts
½ cup dried apricot
¼ cup goji berries
1 tablespoon lemon juice
4 dates
1 lemon, zested
1 tablespoon chia seeds
1 tablespoon hemp seeds

Directions
Soak dates in warm water for 10 minutes to soften then a bit. Drain the water. Combine all ingredients in food processor and process until almost smooth (not completely). Pat bars into baking tray and freeze for 10-15 mins. Cut into bars and store in the refrigerator.

Grated Potato Pancakes

Servings: 4

Ingredients
2 Idaho potatoes (about 1 ¼ pounds)
2 teaspoons canola oil
Coarse salt and freshly ground pepper

Directions
Peel potatoes, and grate on the large holes of a box grater. Place grated potatoes in a clean kitchen towel, and squeeze tightly, removing all excess moisture.

Heat a 10-inch nonstick skillet over medium-high heat and add 1 teaspoon canola oil. When very hot, add grated potatoes, and season with salt and pepper. Use a spatula to press potatoes into a flat, round shape.

Reduce heat to medium, and cook, shaking pan periodically, until pancake is nicely browned, 5 to 7 minutes.

Flip pancake, and add remaining teaspoon of oil, drizzling around the edges of pancake. Gently swirl pan to distribute oil. Season again with salt and pepper. Continue cooking until golden brown and crisp on both sides, 5 to 7 minutes more. Transfer to a cutting board; cut into wedges. Serve immediately.

ENTREES

(lunch or dinner)

Twice-Baked Rosemary Hummus Potatoes
Prep Time: 15 min   Cook Time: 35 min   Servings: 4

Ingredients
8 small Yukon Gold potatoes
1 cup hummus (such as Sabra Classic Hummus)
Sea salt, to taste

Black pepper, to taste
Extra virgin olive oil (for drizzling)
2 tablespoons chopped fresh rosemary

Directions
Preheat your oven to 425°F.
Scrub the potatoes and poke each with a fork 2 to 3 times. Place the whole potatoes on a rimmed baking sheet and bake for approximately 25 to 30 minutes, or until the potatoes are soft. Let cool for 10 minutes.

Carefully slice the potatoes in half lengthwise and scoop out the flesh, leaving about ¼-inch thickness for the potato "bowls". Lightly mash the potato flesh in a bowl. Add the hummus and stir until combined. Season the mixture with salt and pepper, to taste. Using a spoon, divide the potato-hummus filling evenly among the potato "bowls" and drizzle lightly with olive oil. Broil for 5 to 7 minutes or until the tops are golden and crispy; watch carefully as they burn quickly. Sprinkle the hummus potatoes with the rosemary and another pinch of sea salt. Serve immediately.

Zucchini Pasta with Avocado Pesto
Servings: 4

Ingredients
3 medium zucchinis (or spiralized zucchini noodles)
2 cups fresh basil leaves
⅓ cup toasted pine nuts
1 small avocado
2 cloves garlic
1 lemon (juice + zest)
Sea salt to taste
1 can (16 oz) chickpeas
Sun-dried tomatoes to garnish

Directions
Step One: The Zucchini Noodles

Slice off the top and bottom of the zucchini. Then, using a mandolin with a julienne attachment or a julienne peeler, slice into thin pasta-like strips and set aside.

Step Two: The Pesto

In a food processor, combine the basil, pine nuts, avocado, garlic, lemon juice and sea salt. Process until smooth, then taste and adjust any ingredients as necessary. Pesto comes out differently every time, so don't be afraid to throw in more basil, garlic, or salt. You can even add a little water if the sauce is too thick.

Step Three: Toss

Add the zucchini noodles to a bowl and toss with the pesto. Then, add in the chickpeas and sun-dried tomatoes and toss again. Transfer to serving plates and garnish each plate with a sprig of basil.

Roasted Fingerling Potatoes with Asparagus & Green Beans
Servings: 2-4

Ingredients
12 fingerling potatoes
Handful of asparagus spears, woody ends trimmed
Handful of green beans, ends trimmed
1 to 2 tablespoons olive oil
Sea salt and fresh cracked pepper, to taste

Directions
Preheat the oven to 400 degrees. Par-cook the fingerling potatoes for 5 to 6 minutes in a large pot of boiling water. Remove from water and let cool. Line a baking sheet with tin foil for easier clean up then spray with cooking spray. Slice the potatoes into half, lengthwise and put on the baking sheet, drizzle with half of the olive oil and season with salt and pepper to taste.

Bake for 10 to 15 minutes or until golden brown. While the potatoes are cooking, toss the asparagus and green beans with remaining olive oil and season with salt and pepper to taste. Remove the potatoes from oven and toss the asparagus and green beans on the baking sheet with the potatoes. Return to the oven and cook for an additional 4-5 minutes or until the veggies are tender but still a bit crisp. Enjoy!

Spaghetti Squash with Marinara
Servings: 4

Ingredients
1 2-lb spaghetti squash
3 tablespoons extra-virgin olive oil
1 (32-oz.) jar sugar-free marinara sauce
½ teaspoon sea salt
½ teaspoon black pepper
½ cup loosely packed basil leaves, sliced

Directions
Preheat oven to 425 degrees F.
While oven is preheating, cut the squash in half. Remove the seeds and pulp from the center.

Brush the olive oil over the cut side, sprinkle with salt and pepper, and lay on a parchment lined baking sheet cut side down. Bake for 60 minutes.
A few minutes before squash is done, pour marinara in a medium saucepan and heat over medium heat until hot throughout.

When squash is done, scrape the flesh with a fork so the noodles come off, and divide between 4 plates. Top with the marinara and basil before serving.

Vegetable Stir Fry
Prep time: 10min   Cook time: 34min   Servings: 2-4

Ingredients
½ cup brown rice (100 g)
1 cup red cabbage (80 g)
½ head of broccoli
½ red bell pepper
½ zucchini
2 tbsp extra virgin olive oil
4 cloves of garlic
1 handful fresh parsley
1 red chili pepper
2 tbsp tamari or soy sauce
Sesame seeds for garnish (optional)

Directions
Cook the brown rice according to package directions. Boil water, then add the veggies (chopped). Cook for 1 or 2 minutes. Drain the veggies and set aside. Heat the oil in the wok and add the garlic, chili pepper and parsley (finely chopped). Cook over high heat for 1 or 2 minutes stirring occasionally. Add the vegetables, the rice and the tamari. Cook for about 1 or 2 minutes. Add some sesame seeds for garnish (optional).

Wild Rice Burrito Bowl

Ingredients

For the burrito bowl
1½ heaping cups iceberg lettuce, chopped
½ cup cooked wild rice
2 tbsp salsa
2 tbsp corn
2 tbsp refried beans
¼ avocado, sliced or diced
roasted chickpeas

For the dressing:
¾ cup almond milk
2 tbsp olive oil

¾ ripe avocado, diced
1 green onion, sliced
1 tbsp fresh cilantro
1 small clove garlic, minced
1 tbsp lime juice
½ tsp lime zest
¼ tsp each salt, freshly ground pepper, ground cumin and chili powder

To assemble the bowl:
Add the lettuce to the bottom of a serving bowl, add rice and other
desired toppings then drizzle with cilantro-lime avocado dressing.

For the dressing:
In a blender, combine Almond Breeze, olive oil, avocado, green onion,
cilantro, garlic, lime juice, lime zest, salt, pepper and cumin; blend until
smooth. Refrigerate until serving.

Roasted Potato Veggie Casserole
Prep Time: 10min   Cook Time: 1hr   Servings: 4

Ingredients
2 lbs baby red potatoes, halved
1 corn on the cob, husk on
1 red bell pepper, diced
1 orange bell pepper, diced
1 green bell pepper, diced
½ teaspoon cumin
¼ teaspoon ancho chili pepper
1 tablespoon coarse salt
1 teaspoon pepper
1 tablespoon fresh dill, minced + extra roughly chopped to garnish
Green onion, thinly sliced to garnish
3 tablespoons olive oil

Directions
Preheat oven to 400°F.
Toss potatoes, bell peppers, cumin, ancho chili pepper, salt, pepper,
minced dill, and olive oil until coated on a roasting pan. Spread the

vegetables out into a single layer, leaving an empty space for the corn on the cob. Place the corn on the cob, husk still on, in the empty space.

Put the pan on a middle rack in the oven and bake for 30 minutes. Remove the corn on the cob and set aside. Put the pan back in the oven and cook for another 30 minutes, or until potatoes are tender.

While vegetables continue to cook, remove the husk from the corn and slice off the kernels.

When the potatoes are tender enough to be pierced with a fork, remove the pan from the oven. Stir in the corn kernels and add the remaining fresh dill and green onion to garnish.

Zucchini Pepper Stir Fry
Prep time: 10min   Cook time: 10min   Servings: 2

Ingredients
1 tbsp sesame oil
1 clove garlic, minced
½ cup onion, sliced small
2 cups sweet bell pepper, seeded, sliced in thin strips
1 poblano pepper, seeded, sliced in thin strips
2 cups zucchini, sliced in thin strips
2 cup brown rice, cooked

For the sauce:
2 ½ tbsp soy sauce, low sodium
1 tsp. sesame oil
2 tsp Asian Chili Paste
1 tsp Dijon mustard

Directions
Cook rice according to direction.
In a large fry pan, over medium-low heat, add 1 tablespoon of sesame oil. Heat oil for about 30 seconds, add garlic, and cook for 1 minute. Add onion and peppers, stirring occasionally and cook for about 4 minutes.

Add zucchini and cook until slightly tender, but still firm, stirring occasionally. Turn off heat and stir in sauce. Divide, rice between two bowls, and evenly divide vegetables. For a pinch of heat, I added sriracha sauce to the stir-fry.

To make sauce:
In a bowl, add soy sauce, sesame oil, chili paste and mustard; mix until combined.

<u>SIDES</u>

Garlic Mushroom Quinoa

<u>Ingredients</u>
1 cup quinoa
1 tablespoon olive oil
1-pound cremini mushrooms, thinly sliced
5 cloves garlic, minced
½ teaspoon dried thyme

<u>Directions</u>
Kosher salt and freshly ground black pepper, to taste
In a large saucepan of 2 cups water, cook quinoa according to package instructions; set aside.

Heat olive oil in a large skillet over medium high heat. Add mushrooms, garlic and thyme, and cook, stirring occasionally, until tender, about 3-4 minutes; season with salt and pepper, to taste. Stir in quinoa until well combined. Serve immediately.

Roasted Sweet Potatoes & Brussels Sprouts
Servings: 6-8

<u>Ingredients</u>

1-pound Brussels sprouts, trimmed
1 large sweet potato (1 pound)
2 cloves garlic, smashed
⅓ cup olive oil
1 teaspoon cumin
¼ or ½ teaspoon garlic salt
1 teaspoon salt
pepper to taste
1 tablespoon red wine vinegar
fresh thyme, to garnish

Directions
Preheat your oven to 400 degrees F. Trim your Brussels by cutting off the little brown end. If there are any yellow leaves, pull them off. Cut any large ones in half. Add to a large bowl. Peel your sweet potato and chop into 1-2-inch pieces. Add to the large bowl. Smash 2 cloves of garlic and add it to the bowl. Pour ⅓ cup olive oil over the vegetables. Add cumin, garlic salt, salt, and pepper to taste. Stir to coat.

(Line a large sheet pan with foil if you want super easy cleanup)

Drizzle a little olive oil onto the sheet pan and rub it all over the pan (or foil) with your hand. Or you could spray it really well with nonstick spray. Pour the veggies onto the pan.

Roast at 400 for about 40-45 minutes. The veggies are done when they are brown, and a fork can slide into them easily.

Place the veggies in a serving bowl and toss with 1-2 tablespoons red wine vinegar to taste. Garnish with fresh thyme if you want. Eat hot!

Grilled Coconut-Glazed Corn

Ingredients
¾ cup unsweetened coconut milk
1 bay leaf
¼ tsp. salt

4 ears sweet corn, husked or husk stripped back and tied together to form handle

Directions
Combine coconut milk, bay leaf, and salt in small saucepan over medium heat. Remove pan from heat and let mixture cool to room temperature. Preheat grill to high. When ready to cook, brush grill grate clean and apply thin coat of oil to grate. Place corn on hot grate; start basting with coconut milk mixture after a few minutes. Baste several times as it grills until nicely browned on all sides, 2 to 3 minutes per side, 8 to 12 minutes in all, turning with tongs. Baste corn one final time, transfer to platter or plates, and serve.

Note
The handle idea is cute in theory but mine burnt on the grill and flew everywhere so if you tie the husks back and hang them off the grill, so they don't burn or just take the husks off all together.

Easy Zucchini Chips
Prep Time: 10 min   Cook Time: 2 hours   Servings: 3-5

NOTE: Works best if you have a mandolin or veggie slicer

Ingredients
1 large zucchini
2 tbsp olive oil
Kosher salt

Directions
Preheat oven to 225 degrees Fahrenheit. Line two large baking sheets (I used two 17″ baking sheets) with silicon baking mats or parchment paper.

Slice your zucchini on a mandolin. Place the slices on a sheet of paper towels and take another paper towel and sandwich the zucchini slices and press on them. This helps draw out the liquid, so it'll cook a bit faster.

Line up the zucchini slices on the prepared baking sheet tightly next to each other in a straight line, making sure not to overlap them. In a small bowl, pour your olive oil in and take a pastry brush to brush the olive oil on each zucchini slice. Sprinkle salt throughout the baking sheet.

Notes
Do NOT over-season, in fact, it's better to use less salt initially because the slices will shrink; so, if you over-season, it'll be way too salty! You can always add more later.

Bake for 2+ hours until they start to brown and aren't soggy and are crisp. Let cool before removing and serving. Keep in an airtight container for no more than 3 days.

Coconut Lime Quinoa
Prep Time: 5 min   Cook Time: 40 min   Servings: 6-8

Ingredients
1 cup quinoa, rinsed if necessary
1 (13.66-oz.) can of coconut milk
¼ cup water
¼ teaspoon salt
1 small lime, zested and juiced

Directions
Check the quinoa package to see if your quinoa needs rinsed. If it does, pour 1 cup of quinoa into a fine mesh strainer and rinse thoroughly with cold water. Place quinoa, canned coconut milk, water, and salt into the rice cooker. The rice cooker will beep after about 30 minutes. For a standard rice cooker without all of the bells and whistles, one cooking cycle should be enough to do it. Note that you should let the quinoa set for about 4-5 minutes after it's done cooking and then fluff it. Stir in the zest and juice of one small lime, and it's ready to serve.

-OR-

To cook quinoa on your stovetop, simply follow the instructions for rinsing and place all of the ingredients in a saucepan. Bring the mixture to a boil, cover with a lid, and simmer on low for 15 minutes. Let the quinoa set for about 4-5 minutes after it's done cooking and then fluff it. Then stir in the lime zest and juice.

Note
If you substitute coconut milk beverage for the canned coconut, use 2 cups and omit the water.

Oven Roasted Sweet Potato Fries
Prep Time: 15 min.

Ingredients
Sweet potatoes (your desired amount)

Directions
Cut your sweet potatoes into fries or wedges. Coat them with olive oil. Sprinkle them with Chipotle Pepper, this gives it a nice kick! Set your oven to 400 and let them cook until they are soft.

Optional: you can add cinnamon to give it a sweet and spicy feel.

Cilantro Edamame Hummus
Prep Time: 15 min.   Servings: 8

Ingredients
1 (12 oz.) package frozen shelled edamame (green soybeans)
2 cloves garlic
½ cup tahini
½ cup water
½ cup packed cilantro leaves
¼ cup lemon juice
3 tablespoons extra-virgin olive oil

1 teaspoon kosher salt
¾ teaspoon ground cumin
⅛ teaspoon cayenne pepper

Directions
Place edamame into a large pot and cover with salted water. Place over medium-low heat, bring to a simmer, and cook until tender, about 5 minutes; drain.

Puree garlic in food processor until minced. Add edamame, tahini, water, cilantro, lemon juice, olive oil, kosher salt, cumin, and cayenne pepper; blend until smooth.

Flatbread

Ingredients
2 ½ cups whole grain flour (brown rice, spelt, whole wheat, etc.)
2 tablespoons flaxseed meal (optional)
1 teaspoon dried crushed rosemary
1 teaspoon salt
1 cup warm water
1 tablespoon extra-virgin olive oil
½ teaspoon dried basil
½ teaspoon garlic powder
½ teaspoon dried parsley

Directions
Mix flour, flaxseed meal, rosemary, salt, and water in a food processor until dough forms a ball. Turn dough onto a floured work surface and knead for 5 minutes. Transfer to a bowl and cover tightly with plastic wrap. Let dough rest at room temperature 30-60 minutes.

Preheat oven to 400 degrees. Roll dough out to ¼-inch thickness to cover an oiled 11 x 17-inch baking sheet. With a fork, poke holes all across the dough. Mix olive oil, basil, and garlic powder in a small bowl, and stir well. Use a basting brush to spread oil mixture across dough. Score (make shallow cuts without separating into pieces) with a knife into 12 (3 x 3 ½-inch) squares with a knife. Bake 15-20 minutes or until slightly crispy and remove from oven.

Let cool on baking sheet 10 minutes before cutting and serving. Yield: 4 servings (serving size: 2 pieces)

Notes
Flaxseed meal is a powder made from ground flaxseeds. It can be found in health food stores and some grocery stores. Instead of buying flaxseed meal, you can also grind whole flaxseeds at home by using a coffee or seed grinder.

SNACKS

Homemade Tortilla Chips
Prep Time: 15 min   Cook Time: 12 min   Servings: 4-6
Ingredients
15 fresh yellow corn tortillas
2 TBS olive oil, more for brushing on baking sheet
1 TBS lime juice
salt to taste

Directions
Preheat oven to 375 degrees F (190 degrees C). Brush two large baking sheets with olive oil or use cooking spray. In a small bowl, mix 2 tablespoons of oil and 1 tablespoon of lime juice together. Brush oil on one tortilla, making sure to cover the entire surface. Stack another tortilla on top and brush on oil mixture. Continue until you get have about 7 or 8 tortillas in a stack. Cut tortillas in half. Cut each half into small triangles. Set aside.

Brush oil on remaining tortillas and cut into triangles. Arrange tortilla pieces on baking sheet in a single layer. They can be lined right next to each other as they'll shrink once baked. Sprinkle salt all over tortilla pieces.

Bake for 8 to 12 minutes, or until the chips are golden. Depending on the size of your baking sheets, you may need to bake everything in two batches.

Note
Let chips cool before serving. Store chips in an airtight container. They should stay crispy for 1 to 2 weeks.

Homemade Guacamole

Ingredients
2 ripe avocados
¼ onion, finely chopped
1 jalapeno, finely chopped (optional)
Chopped Cilantro
Lime Juice (to taste)
Salt to taste
½ tomato, finely chopped

Directions
Peel the avocado and remove the core. Mash the avocado in a molcajete until it reaches your desired consistency. Add the onion, jalapeno, cilantro and tomato and mix well. Add lime juice and salt to taste.

Fresh Homemade Salsa
Prep Time: 5 min   Servings: 5 cups

Ingredients
4 ripe tomatoes, cored and quartered
1 red onion, peeled and quartered
3 garlic cloves, peeled
3 jalapenos, stemmed and seeded (You can substitute 1-2 habanero or serrano peppers.)
⅓ cup fresh cilantro
3 tablespoons fresh lime juice

1 tablespoon ground cumin
2-3 teaspoons sugar
1 ½ teaspoons salt
15 oz. can crushed San Marzano tomatoes
4.5 oz. can diced green chilies (mild, medium, or hot)

Directions
Place the fresh tomatoes, onion, garlic, peppers, lime juice, cumin, sugar, and salt in a food processor. Pulse until the contents are fine and well blended. Pour in the crushed tomatoes and green chilies. Puree until mostly smooth. Refrigerate until ready to serve.

Trail Mix
Servings: 12

Ingredients
1 cup whole raw almonds or Cinnamon-Roasted Almonds
1 cup cashew halves & pieces
1 cup walnut halves
½ cup golden raisins
½ cup raisins
¼ cup raw sunflower seed kernels
¼ cup raw pumpkin seeds (pepitas)

Directions
Mix ingredients together, and store in an airtight container for 2 weeks at room temperature or 1 month in refrigerator. Try adding fresh fruit; it works great as a topping, though it's optional.

Almond Butter Bites
Prep Time: 10 min   Servings: 6-8

Ingredients
½ cup almond butter
¼ cup raw sunflower seeds
¼ cup raisins
¼ cup chopped almonds
2 tablespoons unsweetened shredded coconut
¼ teaspoon cinnamon

Directions
Mix all ingredients in a bowl until well combined. Use a ½ tablespoon measuring spoon or a large melon ball scoop to form mixture into small balls. Place in an 8 by 8-inch baking dish and freeze until firm. Serve frozen or just slightly thawed.

Roasted Buffalo Chickpeas
Prep time: 5 mins   Cook time: 35 mins   Total time: 40 mins
Serves: 4

Ingredients
1 (16 oz.) can garbanzo beans
½ c. hot sauce (I prefer Franks)
½ teaspoon garlic powder
1 teaspoon sea salt

Directions
Preheat oven to 425°. Drain garbanzo beans, dump onto clean kitchen towel. Top with 2 sheets of paper towel and roll chickpeas to dry. Add in remaining ingredients and toss. Spread onto line baking sheet. Bake 30-40 minutes (check at 30).

Green Monster Pops

Ingredients
1 cup spinach
½ cup kale leaves chopped (remove the tough stems)

3 bananas
1 whole pineapple, peeled and chopped
1½ – 2 cups water

<u>Directions</u>
Combine spinach, kale bananas, and pineapple in a blender and puree, add water; puree a second time. Pour into pop molds or small cups add Popsicle sticks and freeze.

Ice pops are a refreshing treat and a fun way to eat your vegetables. You can use any combination of fruits and vegetables so be creative.

Plantain Chips
Servings: 4-5   Serving Size: about ½ cup

<u>Ingredients</u>
2 green plantains
2 teaspoons extra-virgin coconut oil, melted
½ teaspoon salt
¼ teaspoon cinnamon

<u>Directions</u>
Preheat oven to 400 degrees. Line an 11 x 17-inch baking sheet with parchment paper.

Trim ends of plantains. Score the plantains vertically in three places without cutting through to the fruit. Remove the peel and discard, along with the trimmed ends. Cut plantains in ¼" slices (should make about 3 cups).

In a large bowl, add plantain chips, coconut oil, salt, and cinnamon. Stir well to coat. Place plantain chips on the baking sheet in rows. Cook 15 minutes. Flip, and then bake another 10-15 minutes. Serve immediately.

<u>Note</u>
If the plantains are fully ripened (peel is black), they'll be too soft to make good chips. Keep in mind that Plantain chips do not get as crispy as potato chips. You may need to remove some chips before the others are

done cooking if they start to brown faster. Store uneaten chips in the refrigerator in a sealed container. To reheat, place in an oven or toaster oven at 400 degrees for about 5-7 minutes or until heated through.

SOUPS

Crockpot Lentil Soup

Prep Time: 10 min   Cook Time: 5-8 hours   Servings: 8

Ingredients

For the crockpot:
2 cups Butternut squash
2 cups Carrots
2 cups Celery
5 cloves Garlic
1 cup Green lentils
2 tsp Herbs de Provence
1 Onion
2 cups Potatoes
¾ cup Split peas, yellow
8 cups Vegetable broth
1 tsp Salt

Add later:
½ cup Olive oil – rosemary olive oil or other herb infused oil is delicious
1 cup Parsley
2 cups Kale

Directions
Place all ingredients in the crockpot. Cover and cook on high for 5-6 hours or low for 7-8 hours.

Place about 4 cups of soup in a blender with the olive oil. Pulse gently until semi-smooth and creamy-looking (the oil will form a creamy emulsion with the soup). Add back to the pot and stir to combine. Stir in the kale and parsley. Turn the heat off and just let everything chill out for a bit before serving. The taste gets better with time and so does the texture!

Carrot, Apple, and Ginger Soup
Servings: 8
Ingredients
½ tablespoon extra-virgin olive oil
½ cup chopped onion
1 clove garlic, minced
1 tablespoon minced fresh ginger root
6 cups Vegetable Broth or water
2 pounds carrots, peeled and cut into 2-inch pieces
2 cups chopped apples, peeled
1 bay leaf
½ teaspoon dried thyme
1 teaspoon salt

Directions
Heat olive oil over medium heat in a large saucepan or stockpot. Add onion and cook until translucent. Mix in garlic and ginger, and cook about 1 minute, stirring constantly. Add vegetable broth, carrots, apples, bay leaf, thyme, salt. Bring to a boil. Reduce heat, cover, and simmer 20 minutes, or until carrots are tender.

Remove from heat and allow soup to cool about 5 minutes. Discard bay leaf. Purée the soup in batches in a food processor or blender. When completely smooth, return to stovetop, and cook another 10 minutes.

Note
I used Fuji apples, but you could use just about any type of apple, depending upon your personal preference.

Japanese Clear Onion Soup
Prep time: 10min   Cook time: 30min   Servings: 4

Ingredients
2 diced onions
6 cups vegetable broth or water
2 diced celery stalks
2 carrots (peeled and diced)
2 garlic cloves (minced)
1 handful button mushrooms (thinly sliced)
1 handful sliced scallions
salt and pepper
soy sauce and Sriracha

Directions
Sauté the onions in a pot in a little bit of oil until slightly browned.
Add the carrot, celery, and garlic and 6 cups of vegetable broth/water.
Bring to the boil and then simmer for 30 minutes.

Season to taste with salt and pepper. Strain the veggies from the broth
and add the mushrooms and scallions before serving.

Quinoa Ratatouille
Prep Time: 10 min.   Cook Time: 30 min.   Servings: 10

Ingredients
1 tbs olive or grapeseed oil
1½ cups diced eggplant (most of the skin removed, but leave a little for
color)
1½ cups zucchini squash, quartered and sliced
2 cloves of garlic, minced
1½ cups sweet onion, chopped
½ cup quinoa
3 bay leaves
1½ tsp dry thyme leaves
6 cups of vegetable stock
3 cups of crushed tomato
¼ cup hot chopped peppers (jarred)

Directions

Toss the eggplant, zucchini, onion and garlic in oil. Then place in a preheated (med-high) Dutch oven or soup pot. Sauté for about 2 minutes, then add quinoa and herbs. Sauté until quinoa is golden brown and veggies have started to caramelize (about 8 more minutes).

Add the stock, then tomatoes and peppers, stir. Once it comes to a rapid boil, reduce heat to simmer and cover. Simmer 20 minutes. Serve with fresh chopped basil.

Potato and Roasted Bell Pepper Soup
Prep and Cook Time: 30 minutes   Servings: 4

Ingredients
2 medium red potatoes, cooked (boiled) and unpeeled
2 tablespoons grape seed or coconut oil
½ onion, chopped
1 yellow, orange, or red bell pepper
1 small bunch of asparagus, sliced
4 cups low sodium vegetable broth
1 teaspoon no-salt seasoning or preferred blend of herbs and spices
a couple dashes of smoked paprika
salt and pepper to taste

Directions
This soup can be done in 30 minutes if you can multitask. While the potatoes are boiling, roast the bell pepper over open flames on a gas stove, turning it every couple of minutes with a pair of tongs to roast all sides. Put the roasted bell pepper in a zip lock bag and set aside. Next, heat a little oil in a pot and sauté the onions until slightly brown and translucent. Season with salt and pepper and dump the onions into the blender. Quickly sauté the sliced asparagus in the same pot for about 30 seconds, add salt and pepper, and spoon them out and set aside for later to use as a garnish.

By the time you finish cooking the onions and asparagus, the bell pepper will be ready to peel. Take it out of the bag and remove the burned skin by wiping it with some paper towel. Remove the seeds and rinse it. Check the potatoes to make sure they are soft and cooked completely. Finally, blend the cooked potatoes, roasted bell pepper, onions, vegetable broth, and seasoning together until smooth. Pour the soup into the pot and add a couple of dashes of paprika and salt and pepper to taste. Serve hot and garnish with sliced asparagus.

Greek Vegetable Stew
Prep Time: 55 min.   Servings: 8

Ingredients
2 tablespoons oil
2 onions, chopped
1 pound green string beans, broken in half
1 package frozen or fresh spinach
4 cups water
6 zucchini, chunked
4 yellow squash, chunked
2 cups celery leaves
4 tomatoes, quartered
1 teaspoon salt
8 slices lemon
1 tablespoon dried oregano
3 tablespoons fresh basil
2 cloves chopped garlic
2 tablespoons lemon juice

Directions
Lightly brown onions in a hot dry skillet in 2 tablespoons oil. Add oregano and garlic, cook 1 minute. Add 4 cups water and tomatoes. Cook 10 minutes. Add remaining ingredients. Cook covered for 40 minutes, stirring occasionally. Serve with a lemon slice in each bowl.

Vegetable Chili
Prep time: 15 min   Cook time: 1 hour 15 min   Servings: 8

Ingredients

1 tbs olive oil
2 cups of diced sweet onion (approx. ¾ of a large Vidalia)
1 Poblano pepper, cut into batons (*narrow 1 inch strips*)
2 cloves of garlic, minced
1 small zucchini squash, diced
1 small yellow summer squash, diced
2 tbs chili powder
1 tsp Kosher salt
1 tsp cumin
1 tsp oregano, dry
1 tsp cilantro, dry
½ tsp smoked paprika
¼ tsp cayenne
¼ tsp white pepper
2 bay leaves
1 (15 oz) can Libby's Pumpkin puree
1 (14-15 oz) can diced tomato (with chilis or without)
1 (14-15 oz) can of low sodium black beans, drained and rinsed
2 tbs chopped pickled jalapeno
3 cups of vegetable stock

Directions
Place Dutch oven or stockpot over med-high heat, add oil, once hot add
the onion, Poblano and garlic, sauté 5 minutes, then add the zucchini
and yellow squash and sauté another 5 minutes. Add the salt and
spices, stir for 1 minute, then add the remaining ingredients. Stir. As
soon as the pot starts to bubble, reduce to simmer and cover, to simmer
for 1 hour.

Serve hot. Garnish with chopped scallions, fresh cilantro or chives. If you
are not vegan, a dollop of rich sour cream makes a nice topping.

Black Bean Soup
Prep Time: 45 min.   Servings: 6

Ingredients
1 tablespoon olive oil
1 large onion, chopped

1 stalk celery, chopped
2 carrots, chopped
4 cloves garlic, chopped
2 tablespoons chili powder
1 tablespoon ground cumin
1 pinch black pepper
4 cups vegetable broth
4 (15 oz.) cans black beans
1 (15 oz.) can whole kernel corn
1 (14.5 oz.) can crushed tomatoes

Directions
Heat oil in a large pot over medium-high heat. Sauté onion, celery, carrots and garlic for 5 minutes. Season with chili powder, cumin, and black pepper; cook for 1 minute. Stir in vegetable broth, 2 cans of beans, and corn. Bring to a boil.

Meanwhile, in a food processor or blender, process remaining 2 cans beans and tomatoes until smooth. Stir into boiling soup mixture, reduce heat to medium, and simmer for 15 minutes.

Potato Soup
Serves: 5

Ingredients
¼ cup plus 2 tablespoons olive oil
1 medium onion
3 leeks sliced
3 large baking potatoes peeled and cut in small pieces
1 box vegetable broth
salt & pepper

Directions
Sauté leeks and onion in olive oil. Cover and cook for 20 minutes. Stir in potato and cook 15 more minutes, covered. Add vegetable broth, 1 teaspoon salt and ¼ tea-spoon pepper. Bring to boil. Reduce heat and

simmer 1 – 2 hours. You can either cool and blend in batches in the blender or use a potato masher right in your pot.

Garden Vegetable Soup

Ingredients
4 tablespoons olive oil
2 cups chopped leeks, white part only
2 tablespoons finely minced garlic
2 cups carrots, peeled and sliced into rounds (about 2 medium carrots)
2 cups peeled and diced potatoes
2 cups fresh green beans, broken or
cut into ¾" pieces
2 quarts vegetable broth
4 cups tomatoes, peeled, seeded, and chopped
2 ears corn, kernels removed
½ teaspoon freshly ground pepper
¼ cup packed chopped fresh parsley leaves
2 teaspoons freshly squeezed lemon juice

Directions
Heat the olive oil in a large, heavy-bottomed stockpot over medium low heat. Once hot, add the leeks, garlic, and a pinch of salt and sauté until they begin to soften, approximately 7 to 8 minutes. Add the carrots, potatoes, and green beans and continue to cook for 4 – 5 more minutes, stirring occasionally. Add the stock, increase the heat to high, and bring to simmer.

Once simmering, add the tomatoes, corn kernels, and pepper. Reduce heat to low, cover, and cook until the vegetables are fork tender, approximately 25 to 30 minutes.

Remove from heat and add the parsley and lemon juice. Season to taste with kosher salt. Serve immediately.

Crockpot Vegetarian Split Pea Soup

Ingredients
2 cups green split peas
8 cups water
vegetable broth
2 potatoes, chopped
2 ribs celery, chopped (optional)
2 carrots, sliced
1 onion, diced
2 cloves garlic, minced
1 tsp dry mustard
1 tsp cumin
1 tsp sage
1 tsp thyme
3 bay leaves
salt and pepper to taste

Directions
Combine all ingredients in a crock pot or slow cooker. Cover and cook on low for at least 4 hours, or until peas are soft. Remove bay leaves before serving and adjust seasonings to taste. Makes 8 servings of soup.

Basil Zucchini Soup
Servings: 6   Serving size: 1 cup

Ingredients
1 ½ pounds zucchini, peeled
2 tablespoons extra-virgin olive oil, divided
½ cup chopped onions
2 cloves garlic, minced
4 cups water
1 (15-oz.) can chickpeas, rinsed & drained
½ tablespoon dried basil
1 teaspoon salt
Toasted sunflower and/or pumpkin seeds

Directions
Cut zucchini into 1-inch cubes and set aside. Heat 1 tablespoon olive oil over medium heat in large saucepan. Add onions and garlic and cook until onions are soft and translucent. Add zucchini and stir in 1 tablespoon olive oil. Cook 3-5 minutes, stirring frequently. Pour in water and bring to a boil. Reduce heat, and simmer 15 minutes.

Remove zucchini with a slotted spoon, and place in food processor. Process until mixture is smooth (you may have to do in two batches). Return to saucepan. Place chickpeas in food processor with ½ cup of the soup, and process until texture reaches desired consistency. Add chickpea mixture to saucepan. Stir in basil and salt. Simmer another 15 minutes. Serve with toasted sunflower and/or pumpkin seeds.

Notes: To make this soup chunky instead of smooth, put only half the zucchini and half the chickpeas in the food processor. You can also use oregano instead of basil. Double the recipe, and freeze half for later use.

Black-eyed Peas and Potato Soup
Servings: 6   Serving size: 1 cup

Ingredients
1 tablespoon extra-virgin olive oil
1 cup chopped onion
1 cup sliced carrots
1 cup sliced celery
2 cloves garlic, minced
4 cups Vegetable Broth or water
1 (15-oz.) can black-eyed peas, rinsed & drained
2 cups cubed potatoes
2 tablespoons chopped fresh parsley or 2 teaspoons dried parsley
½ tablespoon dried chives
½ teaspoon salt
⅛ teaspoon cayenne pepper
⅛ teaspoon pepper

Directions

Heat olive oil in a large stock pot over medium heat. Add onions, carrots, and celery. Cook until vegetables are softened. Stir in garlic and cook 1 minute. Add vegetable broth, black-eyed peas, potatoes, parsley, chives, cayenne pepper, salt, and pepper. Bring to a boil. Reduce heat, cover, and simmer 30 minutes.

Notes
For a chunkier soup with a little more texture, place half in a food processor or blender. Substitute black-eyed peas with great northern beans, cannellini beans, or navy beans.

Vegetable Broth

Ingredients
8 cups water
1 onion, quartered
2 carrots, unpeeled and sliced
2 celery stalks, leafy tops included
1 potato, unpeeled and sliced
4 mushrooms, sliced
⅛ cup fresh parsley or ½ tablespoon dried parsley
2 cloves garlic, peeled
1 bay leaf
1 teaspoon thyme
1 teaspoon salt
6 peppercorns

Directions
Place all ingredients in a large stock pot and bring to a boil. Reduce heat, and simmer for about 45 minutes. Strain, cool, and refrigerate. Use as a base for soup. Yield: 8 servings (serving size: about 1 cup)

Note
Experiment with other herbs and spices, such as basil, cumin, oregano, or red pepper flakes. Place strained vegetables in a food processor, and purée until smooth. Add to soups to thicken them.

Other vegetables to use: leeks, parsnips, spinach, tomatoes, turnips, and/or zucchini.

Spinach-Artichoke-Tomato Soup
Servings: 8   Serving size: about 1 cup

Ingredients
1 tablespoon extra-virgin olive oil
1 cup chopped onion
4 cups water
1 (15-oz) can chickpeas, rinsed and drained
1 (14.5-oz) can diced tomatoes, undrained
1 (14-oz) can artichoke hearts, drained and chopped (about 2 cups)
1 (10-oz) package frozen chopped spinach
1 (8-oz) can tomato sauce
2 cloves garlic, minced
1 teaspoon dried basil
1 teaspoon dried oregano flakes
1 teaspoon dried parsley
1 teaspoon salt
$\frac{1}{8}$ teaspoon pepper

Directions
Heat olive oil in large saucepan over medium heat. Add onions and cook until soft and translucent. Add water and remaining ingredients. Heat to boiling, and then reduce heat. Simmer uncovered 30 minutes.

Taco Soup
Servings: 8   Serving size: about 1 cup

Ingredients
1 tablespoon extra-virgin olive oil
½ cup diced onion
4 cups Vegetable Broth or water
1 (14.5-oz) can diced tomatoes
1 (15-oz) can black beans, rinsed & drained

1 (15-z) can pinto beans, rinsed, drained, & mashed
1 (15-oz) can corn, drained
½ cup dry polenta
1 tablespoon Taco Seasoning
1 teaspoon salt
⅛ teaspoon pepper

Directions
Heat olive oil in large saucepan over medium heat. Cook onions until soft and translucent. Add broth, tomatoes, black beans, mashed pinto beans, corn, polenta, Taco Seasoning, salt, and pepper. Heat to boiling. Reduce heat and cook 30 minutes.

Note
Substitute 1 ½ cups cooked brown rice for polenta. Place corn in a food processor and pulse a few times for a cream-style texture. Use kidney beans instead of black or pinto beans.

Butternut Squash and Sweet Potato Soup
Servings: 6   Serving size: about 1 cup

Ingredients
½ tablespoon extra-virgin olive oil
½ cup chopped onion
4 cups water or Vegetable Broth
1 pound butternut squash, peeled & cut into 1-inch cubes
1 pound sweet potatoes, peeled & cut into 1-inch cubes
1 teaspoon fresh minced ginger root or ½ teaspoon ground ginger
½ teaspoon salt
⅛ teaspoon allspice
⅛ teaspoon cinnamon
⅛ teaspoon nutmeg

Directions
Heat olive oil over medium heat and add onions. Cook until onions are soft and translucent. Add water or broth and remaining ingredients to

saucepan and bring to a boil. Reduce heat, and cover. Simmer 30 minutes, or until vegetables are tender.

Remove vegetables with a slotted spoon and place in a food processor or blender. Puree until smooth. (You may need to do this in two batches because filling your processor or blender more than half full could cause the hot soup to pop the lid.) Return to heat and stir well. Use a whisk, if necessary, to smooth out the texture. Cook another 5-10 minutes and serve.

Notes
Use leeks instead of onions (white parts only).

Asian Tofu Stew
Servings: 6-8

Ingredients
½ cup 100% peanut butter
2 cups vegetable broth
2 tablespoons canola oil
1 cup chopped onion
3-4 cloves garlic, minced
1 cup chopped green bell pepper
1 cup chopped carrots
2 pounds firm tofu, cut into 1 ½-inch cubes
2 tablespoons soy sauce
1 teaspoon Five Spices
1 cup diced tomatoes
1 bay leaf
½ teaspoon thyme
½ teaspoon ground ginger
1 tablespoon lemon juice
6-8 cups cooked brown rice

Directions
Whisk together the peanut butter and vegetable broth in a medium bowl until well blended. Season the tofu with soy sauce and Five Spices.
Heat the oil in a large stew pot over medium heat. Add the onion, garlic, bell pepper and carrots. Sauté until the onions are translucent. Add the

tofu and continue to cook, stirring often, until browned on all sides. Add the peanut butter mixture, tomatoes with liquid, thyme, bay leaf, ginger and lemon. Stir well. Bring to a boil. Reduce heat to low and simmer, stirring occasionally for about 20 or until the vegetables are tender. Season to taste with salt and pepper. Serve hot over cooked rice.

Cabbage Soup
Cook Time: 10 minutes   Serving size: 3-4

Ingredients
1 teaspoon olive oil

½ cup chopped onion
1 clove of garlic, crushed
4 cups cabbage, coarsely chopped
4 cups water or vegetable stock
1 bay leaf
½ teaspoon salt + pepper to taste

Directions
Heat oil in a medium soup pot and sauté onion & garlic for 2 minutes. Add cabbage, cook and stir for a minute. Add water or stock, bay leaf, salt, and pepper to taste. Bring to a boil, reduce heat, cover and simmer for 10 minutes.

Note
Try adding a chopped carrot for a fuller meal. To give it a little kick, try adding a chopped jalapeno.

Red Bean Soup
Serving size: 6

Ingredients
1 tablespoon olive oil
1 ½ cups chopped yellow onions

¼ cup chopped green bell peppers
1 tablespoon minced garlic
4 bay leaves
2 cups dried red kidney beans, soaked overnight
1 tablespoon Special Seasoning,
2 quarts vegetable stock
1 teaspoon salt
3 tablespoons chopped parsley
1 cup diced carrots
1 ½ cups cooked long-grain brown rice, warm
6 tablespoons chopped green onions

Directions
Heat the oil in a large heavy pot over high heat. Add the onions, bell peppers, garlic, and bay leaves, and cook, stirring, for 2 minutes.

Add the beans and cook for 2 minutes.

Add the Special Seasoning and stock, stir well, and bring to a boil. Reduce the heat to medium and cook for 1 ½ hours, until beans are tender, stirring occasionally.

Add the salt and parsley, cover the pot, and cook for 15 minutes. Discard the bay leaves. Remove 1 cup of beans from the pot and reserve.

With a hand-held immersion blender, or in batches in a food processor, puree the red beans. Add the reserved beans and stir well.

To serve, ladle a generous cup of the soup into each of 6 bowls. Top each serving with ¼ cup of the rice and 1 tablespoon of green onions.

Corn and Potato Chowder

Ingredients
4 cups corn
2 ½ unsweetened plain soy milk
1 onion chopped
1 sweet bell pepper chopped

2 stalks celery chopped
1 carrot diced
3-4 potatoes peeled and diced
2 cups of vegetable broth
Salt
1 tsp paprika
Cayenne pepper to taste (optional)

Directions
Blend two cups of corn with soy milk in a blender or food processor. Set aside. Sauté the onion, pepper, celery, and carrot in a couple of tablespoons of olive oil around 10 minutes or until tender. Add potatoes. Sauté for about 10 more minutes. Add the corn/soy milk mixture, the rest of the corn, the broth and the spices. Cook for about an hour or until potatoes are tender.

SALADS & DRESSINGS

Basic Oil & Vinegar Dressing

Ingredients
3 tablespoons extra virgin olive oil
1 tablespoon balsamic vinegar (or apple cider vinegar)
Salt & pepper

Directions
Place oil and vinegar in a small bowl and whisk together; season to taste. Pour over your salad and enjoy.

Apple-Cinnamon Salad Dressing

Ingredients
¼ cup extra-virgin olive oil
¼ cup unsweetened apple juice

1 tablespoon fresh lemon juice
1 tablespoon diced red onion
¼ teaspoon cinnamon

Directions
Combine all ingredients in a covered glass jar and shake well. Refrigerate until ready to use.

Note
Use for strawberry spinach salad or other salads—especially ones with fruit and/or berries.

Lemon Olive Oil Dressing

Ingredients
⅓ cup fresh lemon juice (1 large lemon)
¾ cup olive oil
1 – 2 tablespoons tamari (soy) sauce
2 large cloves garlic, crushed
Fresh ground black pepper to taste

Directions
Shake all ingredients in a bottle. Toss with fresh salad greens. Store leftover dressing in the refrigerator.

Creamy Avocado Salad Dressing

Ingredients
1 ripe avocado
1 tablespoon extra-virgin olive oil
1 teaspoon garlic salt
Juice of ½ lemon

Directions

Mash avocado into paste-like consistency. Add garlic salt, lemon juice, and extra-virgin olive oil. Whisk until blended. Spoon over salad and enjoy!

Note
Adjust the quantity of ingredients based on how many people you need to serve. Start out with the smallest amount of oil and adjust from there. Add additional avocados to serve more people and add more oil to make the dressing creamier.

Herbal Vinaigrette

Ingredients
1 clove garlic
2 tablespoons fresh lemon juice
2 teaspoons Dijon mustard
½ cup organic olive oil
¼ teaspoon sea salt
½ teaspoon basil
½ teaspoon marjoram
½ teaspoon parsley
½ teaspoon tarragon
½ teaspoon thyme
⅛ teaspoon cayenne pepper

Directions
Place garlic, lemon juice and Dijon mustard in blender or food processor. Blend briefly. Slowly drizzle olive oil into blender while blender is running. Blend until mixture is combined. Stop and add salt, herbs, and cayenne. Blend briefly again until mixed. Tastes more flavorful when served at room temperature. Refrigerate leftovers.

Creamy Cucumber Dressing

Ingredients

2 cups cut-up cucumbers
1 clove garlic
2 tablespoons chopped onion
3 tablespoons fresh lemon juice
½ teaspoon sea salt
1 teaspoon dried dill
dash cayenne pepper
½ cup organic olive oil

Directions
Peel and cut up cucumbers to equal 2 cups. Place in blender. Add peeled garlic. Slightly chop onion and add to blender. Add lemon juice, salt and cayenne. Blend until combined. Add dill and mix in. Then drizzle in olive oil while blender is mixing on slow speed. Blend until oil is incorporated into dressing. Refrigerate until ready to use.

Orange-Poppy Seed Salad Dressing

Ingredients
¼ cup extra-virgin olive oil
¼ cup orange juice
2 tablespoons fresh lemon juice
1 tablespoon diced red onion
½ teaspoon poppy seeds
¼ teaspoon orange zest
⅛ teaspoon dry mustard
⅛ teaspoon salt

Directions
Combine all ingredients in a covered glass jar and shake well. Refrigerate until ready to use.

Curry Ranch Dressing

Ingredients
1 cup soaked raw cashews*

½ cup fresh filtered water
1 tablespoon fresh lemon or lime juice
½ to 1 teaspoon mild curry powder, to taste
¼ teaspoon organic garlic powder
¼ teaspoon organic onion powder

Directions
Combine the cashews, water, lemon juice, curry, garlic powder, and onion powder in a blender or food processer and blend until smooth and creamy. If the sauce is too thick, add filtered water one tablespoon at a time to thin; pulse after each addition. Season with salt and black pepper to taste. Add the fresh chopped herbs and pulse briefly, just to combine. Adjust seasonings to your liking. Store in a covered glass jar or storage container in the refrigerator. The flavor gets better as it chills. Use as a salad dressing or dip for raw vegetables. Best used within four days.

Note
This recipe calls for organic spices and fresh herbs. If you don't have them available, use regular spices and dried herbs. Dried herbs are more concentrated—use about one-third as much if you use dried.

*For soaked cashews: place 1 cup raw cashews in a glass or ceramic bowl. Cover with fresh filtered water. Cover the bowl with a clean tea towel and let the cashews soak for two hours. Drain and use in recipe.

Clean Ketchup

Ingredients
6 oz. tomato paste
¾ cup water
1½ tablespoons vinegar

Directions
In a small saucepan, combine all ingredients, then stir and simmer over medium heat. Continue to stir until ketchup reaches desired

consistency, approximately 5 minutes. Remove from heat and allow to cool before serving or, even better, refrigerate overnight.

Peach Salsa

Ingredients
1 cup chopped fresh or frozen peaches
1 (4-oz.) can chopped green chilies
2 tablespoons finely diced red onion
2 tablespoons fresh lime juice
1 tablespoon chopped fresh cilantro
⅛ teaspoon salt

Directions
Mix ingredients in a medium-sized bowl and stir well. Refrigerate for about 2 hours or until chilled. Serve. Yield: 6 servings (about ¼ cup each)

Burrito Salad
Servings: 4

Ingredients
2 cups cooked brown rice
1 15 oz can black beans, drained and rinsed
1 7oz can Mexicorn (Mexican corn)
1 onion, thinly sliced
3 bell peppers (red, yellow, green), thinly sliced
1 cup tomato, diced
2 cups romaine lettuce
1 4oz can black olives
2 green onions, sliced
1 avocado, sliced
Fresh cilantro
Fresh lime
Salsa

Directions
Cook rice according to package instructions. Sauté sliced onions and bell peppers over medium heat, stirring frequently, until tender – approximately 10 minutes. Layer rice, beans, and cooked onions and bell peppers in bowl. Top with remaining ingredients (as desired). Use fresh lime juice and/or salsa as a dressing.

Blackberry & Avocado Salad
Servings: 4

Ingredients
4 cups mixed salad greens
1 cup blackberries
1 avocado, peeled, pitted, and cut into 1-inch cubes
1 cup mango, peeled, pitted, and cut into 1-inch cubes
½ cup pecan halves

Directions
In a large bowl, combine salad greens, blackberries, avocado, mango, and pecan halves. Toss, and serve with Orange-Poppy Seed Salad Dressing.

In a large bowl, combine salad greens, blackberries, avocado, mango, and pecan halves. Toss, and serve with Orange-Poppy Seed Salad Dressing.

Optional alternatives
Substitute mango with 1 cup peaches, peeled, pitted, and chopped into 1-inch cubes. Use fresh blueberries instead of blackberries.

Detox Salad
Prep Time: 5min   Servings: 1-2

Ingredients

For the Dressing
1 tablespoon tahini
1 tablespoon lemon juice
Pinch of red pepper flakes
1 teaspoon sesame oil
1 tablespoon rice wine vinegar
1 teaspoon honey
¼ teaspoon salt
¼ teaspoon black pepper
¼ teaspoon oregano
1 clove garlic, minced

For the Salad
1 cup chopped Romaine lettuce
1 cup baby spinach
1 large cucumber, chopped
½ cup shredded carrot
2 green onions, sliced
½ cup blueberries
½ cup avocado, sliced
½ cup snap peas, sliced
1 tablespoon chia seeds

Directions
Combine all the dressing ingredients in a jar with a tight-fitting lid, place lid on tight, and shake until well-combined. Set aside.

Combine the salad ingredients into a large bowl. Drizzle with dressing. Serve immediately.

Spinach Strawberry Salad

Ingredients
1 bunch fresh spinach
1 cup sliced fresh strawberries
½ cup raw pecans
¼ cup balsamic vinegar

½ cup olive oil
salt and ground black pepper to taste

<u>Directions</u>
Combine the spinach, strawberries and pecans in a large bowl. Stir the olive oil into the balsamic vinegar while whisking continuously. Season with salt and pepper. Drizzle the dressing over the salad just before serving.

Salad Ole
Prep Time: 15 min.   Chill Time: 3-4 hours   Servings: 6

<u>Ingredients</u>
2 cups tomatoes, seeded and chopped
1 cup diced zucchini
1 cup frozen corn kernels
⅓ cup chopped green onions
1 avocado – peeled, pitted and diced
⅓ cup picante sauce
2 tablespoons oil
2 tablespoons lemon juice
½ teaspoon garlic salt
¼ teaspoon ground cumin

<u>Directions</u>
In a large bowl, combine the tomatoes, zucchini, corn, green onions, and avocado.

Whisk together the picante sauce, oil, lemon juice, garlic salt, and cumin. Toss gently with the vegetables. Chill 3-4 hours and toss before serving.

Kale, Quinoa, Black Bean Salad

<u>Ingredients</u>

2 cups cooked quinoa (about ¾ cup uncooked)
1 large lemon, zested and juiced (¼ c. juice, 1 tablespoon. zest)
¼ teaspoon coriander
½ teaspoon cumin
1 teaspoon chili paste (or ¼ teaspoon chili flakes)
¼ cup cilantro, chopped
½ cup extra virgin olive oil
¼ cup honey
3 cups thinly shredded kale leaves, raw
1 can black beans, drained and rinsed
1 large carrot, grated
½ red pepper, chopped
2 green onions, chopped
1 avocado, chopped

Directions
Cook quinoa (1 cup quinoa to 2 cups water) according to package directions. Zest and juice lemon into large bowl._Add coriander, cumin, chili paste, cilantro and mix.

Drizzle in olive oil while whisking vigorously. Add honey and mix well.

Chop kale thinly and add to bowl along with the remaining ingredients except avocado. Toss well with dressing. Chop avocado and add at last minute.

Tangled Thai Rainbow Salad
Prep Time:15 mins   Cook Time: 5 mins   Total Time: 20 mins
Servings: 4

Ingredients

For the Salad
2 medium-sized zucchinis
2 medium-sized carrots or 1 medium sweet potato
½ red pepper
1 cup bean sprouts
2 cup shredded kale

½ cup Shredded red cabbage
3 green onions, chopped
1 cup shelled edamame, thawed
½ - ⅔ cup cilantro, chopped
2 radishes, julienned
½ cup shaved almonds or sunflower seeds

For the Peanut Dressing
½ cup natural peanut butter
2 tablespoon apple cider vinegar
1 teaspoon minced or grated ginger
crushed red pepper flakes to taste
¼ cup brown sugar or ¼ c. honey (optional)
¼ teaspoon minced garlic
½ teaspoon chili oil (optional)
1 teaspoon sesame oil
1 c. water (to thin to liking)

Directions for the salad
Spiralize, julienne peel or thinly cut zucchini and carrots into bowl.
Thinly slice red pepper then cut across the slices to make ½ inch pieces.
Add to bowl along with bean sprouts.

Stack kale leaves and thinly slice across the leaves to make shreds and
add to bowl. Thinly slice and then chop red cabbage. Chop green onions
and add to bowl.

Rinse edamame under warm water until thawed and add to bowl. Add
radishes to bowl. Chop cilantro and add to bowl.

Make Peanut dressing (follows) and add to bowl.

Toss salad well and sprinkle almonds or sesame seeds over top just
before serving.

Directions for the Peanut Dressing
In a small saucepan, whisk all ingredients but water for the Peanut
Dipping Sauce over low heat until heated through.

Drizzle in water until sauce is consistency of mayonnaise and lightens in color.

Southwest Corn & Black Bean Salad

Ingredients
1⅓ cups corn kernels, fresh or frozen
⅓ cup pine nuts
¼ cup lime juice
2 tablespoons extra virgin olive oil
¼ cup chopped fresh cilantro
2 14.5-oz. cans black beans, rinsed
2 cups shredded red cabbage
1 large tomato, diced
½ cup minced red onion

Directions
Place pine nuts in a small dry skillet over medium heat and cook, stirring until fragrant and lightly browned, 2 to 4 minutes. Whisk lime juice, oil, cilantro, salt, and pepper in a large bowl. Add the corn, pine nuts, beans, cabbage, tomato, and onion; toss to coat. Refrigerate until ready to serve. Add freshly ground pepper and salt to taste just before serving.

Beautiful Green Salad

Ingredients
8 cups baby spinach
½ of a medium red onion, sliced and separated into rings
1 cucumber, seeded and cut into ½" chunks
1 large can mandarin oranges
1½ cups naturally sweetened dried cranberries
1 cup roasted sliced almonds
1 cup balsamic salad dressing*

Directions

Place servings of spinach on salad plates. Top with red onion, cucumber chunks, orange slices, cranberries, and sliced almonds in that order. Drizzle with dressing.

Optional: Or you can try the Orange-Poppy Seed Dressing.

Cinnamon-Raisin Carrot Salad
Servings: 10   Serving size: ½ cup

Ingredients for the salad
2 cups peeled, shredded carrots
1 cup shredded red cabbage
1 apple, cored, unpeeled, cut into 1-inch matchsticks (about 1 ½ cups)
½ cup raisins
¼ cup chopped pecans (or walnuts)
2 tablespoons raw sunflower seed kernels

Ingredients for the dressing
⅓ cup unsweetened apple juice
1 teaspoon cinnamon

Directions for the salad
Mix carrots, cabbage, apple, raisins, pecans, and sunflower seeds kernels in a large bowl.

Directions for the dressing
In a smaller bowl, add apple juice and cinnamon. Use a whisk to combine and pour over carrot mixture.

Stir well to coat. Place in refrigerator 1–2 hours or until cool. Serve chilled.

Pineapple-Kiwifruit Salad
Servings: 6   Serving size: about 1 cup

Ingredients
6 cups fresh spinach leaves, torn, stems removed, lightly packed
1 (8-oz) can pineapple tidbits, drained, juice reserved
5-6 kiwifruit, peeled, cut into half moons
¼ cup diced red onion

Directions
Wash spinach leaves well, and place in a large serving bowl. Top spinach with pineapple, kiwifruit, and red onion. Pour pineapple juice overall and toss gently.

SMOOTHIES & JUICES

Blueberry Oatmeal Smoothie

Ingredients
½ medium frozen banana
½ cup fresh or frozen blueberries
¼ cup rolled oats
1 cup almond or coconut milk
Directions
Place all ingredients into a blender and puree until smooth. Pour into a glass and serve with a straw.

Green Power Smoothie
Prep Time: 10 min.   Servings: 4

Ingredients
3 cups ice cubes, or as desired
2 cups baby spinach leaves, or to taste
1 (7 oz.) can crushed pineapple
½ cup water, or to taste
1 banana, broken into chunks
1 orange, peeled and segmented

10 fresh mint leaves, or more to taste
1 lemon, juiced
1 lime, juiced

Directions
Blend ice, spinach, pineapple, water, banana, orange, mint, lemon juice, and lime juice in a blender until smooth.

All-Fruit Smoothie
Prep Time: 10 min.   Servings: 2

Ingredients
1 cup pineapple juice
1 large banana, cut into chunks
1 cup frozen strawberries
1 cup frozen blueberries

Directions
Pour pineapple juice into a blender and add banana, strawberries, and blueberries. Cover and blend until smooth, about 1 minute. Pour into 2 glasses.

Plum Good Smoothie
Servings: 2   Serving size: about 1 cup

Ingredients
1 cup water
1 apple, unpeeled, chopped
1 frozen banana, peeled, sliced
¼ cup dried plums (about 6)
1 tablespoon flaxseed meal
1 tablespoon unsweetened shredded coconut

Directions

Add all ingredients to a blender. Process about 1 minute or until completely smooth.

Note
To prepare banana ahead of time, remove peel and place in a plastic zip top bag until frozen. Add chopped nuts to boost the protein content.

Sunny Mint Smoothie/Juice

Ingredients
1 Apple
2 Oranges
1 Bunch of Mint leaves

Directions for smoothies
Place all ingredients into a blender and puree until smooth. Pour into a glass and serve with a straw. For cooler drinks, add ice with the ingredients.

Directions for juice
Place all ingredients into a juicer. Pour into a glass and serve.

The Hulk Smoothie/Juice

Ingredients
1 Pear
4 Celery Stalks
1 Cucumber
1 Handful of Spinach
3 Lettuce Leaves
1 Lemon

Directions for smoothies
Place all ingredients into a blender and puree until smooth. Pour into a glass and serve with a straw. For cooler drinks, add ice with the ingredients.

Directions for juice
Place all ingredients into a juicer. Pour into a glass and serve.

The Big Bang Smoothie/Juice

Ingredients
2 Pears
1 Apple
1 Handful of Spinach
1 Mango
4 Bananas
Directions for smoothies
Place all ingredients into a blender and puree until smooth. Pour into a glass and serve with a straw. For cooler drinks, add ice with the ingredients.

Directions for juice
Place all ingredients into a juicer. Pour into a glass and serve.

Red Roar Smoothie/Juice

Ingredients
3 Carrots
2 Large Red Beets
2 Apples
1 Lemon
1 Inch Ginger Root

Directions for smoothies
Place all ingredients into a blender and puree until smooth. Pour into a glass and serve with a straw. For cooler drinks, add ice with the ingredients.

Directions for juice
Place all ingredients into a juicer. Pour into a glass and serve.

Spicy Lemonade Smoothie/Juice

Ingredients
2 Lemons
3 Apples
1 Tsp Cayenne Pepper

Directions for smoothies
Place all ingredients into a blender and puree until smooth. Pour into a glass and serve with a straw. For cooler drinks, add ice with the ingredients.

Directions for juice
Place all ingredients into a juicer. Pour into a glass and serve.

Very Berry Good Smoothie/Juice

Ingredients
1 Handful of Raspberries
1 Handful of Spinach
1 Mango
4 Bananas
1 Pear
1 Apple

Directions for smoothies
Place all ingredients into a blender and puree until smooth. Pour into a glass and serve with a straw. For cooler drinks, add ice with the ingredients.

Directions for juice
Place all ingredients into a juicer. Pour into a glass and serve.

Liquid Sunshine Smoothie/Juice

Ingredients

1 Pineapple
3 Apples
3 Lettuce Leaves
2 Lemons

Directions for smoothies
Place all ingredients into a blender and puree until smooth. Pour into a glass and serve with a straw. For cooler drinks, add ice with the ingredients.

Directions for smoothies
Place all ingredients into a juicer. Pour into a glass and serve.

Morning Joe Smoothie/Juice

Ingredients
1 Handful Raspberries
1 Handful Spinach
1 Mango
4 Bananas
1 Pear
1 Apple

Directions for smoothies
Place all ingredients into a blender and puree until smooth. Pour into a glass and serve with a straw. For cooler drinks, add ice with the ingredients.

Directions for juice
Place all ingredients into a juicer. Pour into a glass and serve.

DESSERT

Watermelon Coconut Milkshake

Ingredients
1 ½ cups cubed (1-inch chunks) seedless watermelon, frozen
1 cup coconut milk
1 teaspoon vanilla extract
unsweetened coconut flakes, for garnish

Directions
Place all ingredients into a blender and puree until smooth. Sprinkle coconut flakes on top, if desired. Pour into a glass and serve with a straw.

Banana Coconut Ice Cream
Prep Time: 5 min   Freeze Time: 5-6 hours   Servings: 8-12
Ingredients
2 (14-oz.) cans coconut milk
2 bananas, peeled, sliced
¼ cup Date Honey or 6-7 soaked dates, drained

Directions
Place ingredients in a food processor or blender. Mix until smooth. Place in a covered glass bowl in freezer 5-6 hours or until firm (but not solid). If the mixture gets too hard, set it out on the kitchen counter to thaw until soft enough to serve.

Note
If using whole dates instead of Date Honey, soak dates in ¼ cup water. Let sit at room temperature 2 hours or until softened. Drain water and place dates in food processor with coconut milk and bananas. Process until smooth, and freeze.

To add a strawberry flavor, mix in 2 cups sliced strawberries.

Peanut Butter & Oatmeal Cookies
Total Time: 30 minutes

Ingredients
2 medium ripe bananas, mashed
1 cup of uncooked quick oats
2 tbsp <u>natural</u> peanut butter
Polaner All Fruit spreadable fruit (choose any flavor)

Directions
Preheat oven to 350°F. Spray a non-stick cookie sheet with cooking spray or use a Silpat. Combine the mashed bananas and peanut butter in a medium bowl.

Add the oats and mix until thoroughly combined.
Place batter by tablespoons on the cookie sheet, making an indent with the back of the measuring spoon. Repeat until you have 16 cookies.

Bake 15 minutes or until golden. Remove from oven and top each with ¼ teaspoon spreadable fruit

Blueberry Mango Sorbet
Servings: 4   Serving size: about ½ cup

Ingredients
2 cups frozen blueberries
2 cups frozen mango chunks (1-inch cubes)

Directions
Mix blueberries and mango in a blender until smooth, or feed through a juicer with the blank attachment in place.

Almond Cookies
Servings: 14   Serving size: 1 cookie

Ingredients for Date Honey
1 cup pitted dates (about 6-8 Medjool or 18-20 Deglet Noor)
1 cup water
½ teaspoon cinnamon

Directions
Pour dates and water into a small saucepan, making sure dates are completely covered (add additional water if necessary). Bring to a boil over high heat. Reduce heat to low and simmer 45-60 minutes or until dates are very soft and broken down. Remove from heat and allow to cool slightly for about 15 minutes. Pour mixture (including liquid) into a blender or food processor and puree until completely smooth. Sprinkle in cinnamon and stir well. Store in a sealed container in refrigerator.

Notes
Here is a brief description of three most popular dates.
- Medjool – largest, sweetest date that is soft and tender
- Deglet Noor – semi-dry chewy "bread" date with a nutty flavor; not as sweet as other dates; smaller than the Medjool
- Pakistani – semi-dry date that is very similar to the Deglet Noor but is slightly smaller.

Ingredients for Almond cookies
1 cup almond meal or flour
⅓ cup almond butter
¼ cup unsweetened orange juice
2 tablespoons flaxseed meal
¼ cup + 3 tablespoons Date Honey
2 tablespoons sliced almonds

Directions for Almond cookies
Preheat oven to 350 degrees. In a large bowl, mix almond meal, almond butter, orange juice, and flaxseed meal. Lightly rub an 11 x 17-inch baking sheet with olive oil. Place dough on baking sheet and flatten with your hands to about ⅛-inch thickness. Use a circle cookie cutter about the size of a ⅓ cup measuring scoop to cut out cookies (or use the measuring cup itself). Spread about ½ tablespoon Date Honey on each cookie, and top with 3-4 sliced almonds. Bake 10 minutes. Remove from oven, and transfer cookies to a wire rack to cool.

Notes
Use unsweetened applesauce as a topping instead of Date Honey. Omit the toppings, and crumble baked cookie over fresh fruit.

Date Honey Banana Pops
Servings: 8   Serving size: 1 banana pop

Ingredients for Date Honey
1 cup pitted dates (about 6-8 Medjool or 18-20 Deglet Noor)
1 cup water
½ teaspoon cinnamon

Directions
Pour dates and water into a small saucepan, making sure dates are completely covered (add additional water if necessary). Bring to a boil over high heat. Reduce heat to low and simmer 45-60 minutes or until dates are very soft and broken down. Remove from heat and allow to cool slightly for about 15 minutes. Pour mixture (including liquid) into a blender or food processor and puree until completely smooth. Sprinkle in cinnamon and stir well. Store in a sealed container in refrigerator.

Notes
Here is a brief description of three most popular dates.
- Medjool – largest, sweetest date that is soft and tender
- Deglet Noor – semi-dry chewy "bread" date with a nutty flavor; not as sweet as other dates; smaller than the Medjool
- Pakistani – semi-dry date that is very similar to the Deglet Noor but is slightly smaller.

Ingredients for Banana Pops
4 medium bananas (7-8 inches long), peeled and halved
8 wooden popsicle sticks
½ cup chopped nuts (almonds, pecans, walnuts, etc.)
2 ½ tablespoons unsweetened shredded coconut

Directions

Cut bananas in half. Line an 11 x 17-inch baking sheet with parchment or wax paper. Insert a popsicle stick into one end of every banana half. Place bananas on sheet so they're not touching and put in freezer. Freeze at least 2 hours or until firm.

Note
Once you've made the Banana Pops and the Date Honey, you're ready to add toppings. Remove pops from freezer. Using a butter knife, spread a thin layer of Date Honey on all sides of each banana piece.

Place chopped nuts and unsweetened shredded coconut on a plate. Roll banana pops in the toppings. Use your fingers to push toppings into the bananas, if necessary. Place the coated bananas on the parchment paper and freeze for 1-2 hours.

Optional
Other toppings ideas are chia seeds, dried fruit, hemp seeds, nut butter, and sunflower seeds. To cut down on the natural sugar content of this recipe, use half the amount of Date Honey.

Apple Raisin Nut Cookies
Servings: 16   Serving size: about 1 cookie

Ingredients
2 cups chopped apples, unpeeled (about 2 apples)
1 cup brown rice flour
1 cup cashew halves and pieces
1 cup pecan halves
1 cup raisins

Directions
Preheat oven to 350 degrees. Add apples, brown rice flour, cashews, pecans, and raisins to a food processor. Process about 30 seconds for a smooth texture or 15 seconds for a nuttier cookie. Drop by spoonful, two inches apart, on an ungreased 11 by 17-inch baking sheet. Flatten to desired shape. Bake 15 minutes. Let cool on a wire rack.

Note
Substitute walnuts or almonds for pecans. You can also use any whole grain flour in place of the brown rice flour.

Health Benefits Charts

Fruit or Vegetable	Health Benefits				
Aloe Vera	Halts growth of cancer tumors	Boosts blood oxygenation	Heals physical burns and radiation burns	Alkalizes the body	Ends constipation
Apples	Protects your heart	Prevents constipation	Block diarrhea	Improves lung capacity	Cushions joints
Apricots	Combats cancer	Controls bleed pressure	Saves eyesight	Shields against Alzheimer's	Slows aging process
Artichokes	Aids digestion	Lowers cholesterol	Protects your heart	Stabilizes blood sugar	Guards against liver disease
Avocados	Battles diabetes	Lowers cholesterol	Helps stops strokes	Controls blood pressure	Smooths the skin
Bananas	Protects your heart	Quiets a cough	Strengthens bones	Controls blood pressure	Calms upset stomach
Beans	Prevents constipation	Prevents Parkinson's disease	Lowers cholesterol	Combats cancer	Stabilizes blood sugar
Beets	Controls blood pressure	Combats cancer	Strengthens bones	Protects your heart	Aids weight loss
Blackberries	Prevents Parkinson's disease	Reduce heart attack risks	Keeps colon clean	Reverse aging	Prevents wrinkles
Broccoli	Strengthens bones	Saves eyesight	Combats cancer	Protects your heart	Control blood pressure

Cabbage	Combats cancer	Prevents constipation	Promotes weight loss	Protects your heart	Helps with headaches
Cantaloupe	Saves eyesight	Controls blood pressure	Lowers cholesterol	Combats cancer	Supports immune system
Cucumber	Skin health	Healthy hair	Cancer prevention	Mosquito repellant	Helps with headaches
Dates	Diabetes control	Liver protection	Kidney protection	Anti-obesity	Anti-cancer
Kale	Lung decongestant	Kidney & liver detoxification	Increases metabolism	Prevents several cancer types	Anti-aging properties
Lemon	Inhibits cancer	Promotes oral health	Reduces kidney stone formation	Alleviates depression	Controls cholera outbreaks
Mangoes	Free radical scavenging	Immune system boosting	Improves memory	Improves vision and eye health	Boosts red blood cells
Orange	Anti-cancer	Pain killer	Heart health	Anti-hypertensive	Stroke prevention
Pineapple	Anti-cancer	Bone health	Anti-inflammatory	Boots immune system	Digestive aid
Watermelon	Reduces high blood pressure	Reduces heart disease	Super hydrating	Boosts immune	Cleans kidneys

Nuts & Seeds	Health Benefits				
Almonds	Appetite control	Weight control	Bone health	Memory booster	Biotin source
Apricot Seeds	Prevents cancer	Pain in arthritis	Lowers high blood pressure	Resists colds and flu	Hair health
Brazil Nuts	Lower risk of pancreatic cancer	Reduce blood sugar levels	Prevents thyroid enlargement	Prevent reproductive disorders	Protection from tumors

Cashew Nuts	Heart health	Reduce blood pressure	Prevent diabetes	Protects against cataracts	Help form blood cells
Chestnuts	Improves glycemic control	Memory protection	Bowel health	Anemia treatment	Weight loss
Chia Seeds	Protects against heart disease	Aid in weight loss	Energy boost	Protects against diabetes	Reduces joint pain
Cumin Seeds	Help digestive disorders	Antiseptic	Boosts power of liver	Treats asthma and arthritis	Boosts immune system
Flax Seeds	Relief of abdominal pains	Anti-inflammatory	Stabilize hormonal levels	Reduce symptoms of PMS and menopause	Reduce risk of breast & prostate cancer
Grape Seeds	Prevents high blood pressure	Lowers cholesterol	Reduces swelling from injury	Helps eye disease from diabetes	Healing wounds
Hazelnuts	Cardiovascular health	Alzheimer's disease	Rheumatoid arthritis	Cancer prevention	Diabetes
Hemp Seeds	Strengthens immunity	Helps cardiovascular health	Superior source of protein	Improves skin and hair	Cancer treatment
Macadamia Nuts	Lower blood cholesterol levels	Reduce risks of diabetes	Cleans colon	Anemia treatment	Morning sickness relief
Pecans	Source of vitamins A, B, & E	Cardiovascular health	Anti-cancer	Bone & teeth health	Prevents skin problems
Pine Nuts	Suppress your appetite	Boost energy	Heart health	Anti-aging antioxidants	Vision health
Pistachios	Weight loss	Diabetes/insulin	Cancer protective phenolics	Lower blood pressure	Rheumatoid arthritis support
Pomegranate seeds	Rich source of antioxidants	Pumps oxygen in blood	Reduce risk of cancer	Lessens inflammation from arthritis	Reduce risk of heart disease

Pumpkin Seeds	Good source of vitamin B	Fights depression	Boosts mood	Prevent certain kidney stone formation	Fights parasites
Sesame Seeds	Lowers cholesterol	Prevents high blood pressure	Relief for Rheumatoid Arthritis	Protects liver	Good source of calcium
Sunflower Seeds	Helps reduce severity of asthma	Lower high blood pressure	Prevent migraine	Reduce risk of heart attack	Reduce risk of stroke
Walnut	Anti-inflammatory	Prevents heart disease	Prevents liver damage	Brain health	Prevents prostate/breast cancer

Spices	Health Benefits				
Cinnamon	Reduces blood sugar levels	Cancer prevention	Strengthens cardiovascular system	Eases menstrual cycles	Builds immune system
Cumin	Fights diabetes	Helps with digestion	Treats food poisoning	Increases milk flow in nursing mothers	Treat skin problems such as boils, eczema, acne and dry skin
Ginger	Motions sickness/Nausea	Migraines	Heart burn	Help fight cancer	Reduce inflammation
Mint	Treats nausea and indigestion	Headache relief	Prevents mental fatigue	Ease symptoms of IBS	Prevents tooth decay
Onion	Reduce risk of cancer	Lower cholesterol	Lowers risk of heart attacks	Helps treat acne	Treat coughs
Turmeric	Natural liver detoxifier	Speeds wound healing	Relieves headaches	Decongestant	Slows progression of Alzheimer's
Vanilla	Fights cancer	Prevent or treat sickle cell disease	Skin care	Soothes anxiety	Aids in weight loss

Concerns	Ingredients
Arthritis	Carrot, Celery, Pineapple, Lemon
Asthma	Carrot, Spinach, Apple, Garlic, Lemon
Cold	Carrot, Pineapple, Ginger, Garlic
Constipation	Carrots, Apple, Fresh Cabbage
Depression	Carrot, Apple, Spinach, Beet or Noni
Diabetes	Carrot, Spinach, Celery
Eyes	Carrot, Celery
Fatigue	Carrots, Betts, Green Apple, Lemon, Spinach
Headache	Apple, Cucumber, Kale, Ginger, Celery
High blood pressure	Beet, Apple, Celery, Cucumber, Ginger
Indigestion	Pineapple, Carrot, Lemon, Mint
Kidney detox	Carrot, Watermelon, Cucumber, Cilantro
Kidney stone	Orange, Apple, Watermelon, Lemon
Memory loss	Pomegranate, Beet, Grapes
Nervousness	Carrot, Celery, Pomegranate
Stress	Banana, Strawberry, Pear
Ulcer	Cabbage, Carrot, Celery

Week 1:

Preparing Your Heart and Mind

Day 1: Repentance   Date: _____ /_____/_____

When you start a fast, it is important to start your fast with honesty and transparency. One sure way to do this is to admit that you are not perfect... at all! However, strive for greatness and depend on God for edification. Repentance is not only feeling sorrowful for the wrong that you've done, although it plays a part in your humility. Repentance also means to have a changed mind. It is possible to feel sorrow about something you've done, but does that really stop you from doing it again? True repentance means you have a changed mind against the wrong you've done. If you were faced with that opportunity again, you would do differently because you no longer believe that your last action was an appropriate one.

So, today we will go to the Father for personal repentance with a contrite heart. Ask God to cleanse you of all known and unknown sin and help you in every area as you dedicate and consecrate yourself to Him during this time of fasting and prayer. Ask the Holy Spirit to search your heart and reveal any areas of unconfessed sin. Acknowledge those offenses (aloud) to the Lord and thank Him for His forgiveness.

Scripture References:

"Search me, O God, and know my heart; try me, and know my anxieties; and see if *there is any* wicked way in me and lead me in the way everlasting." (Psalm 129:23-24, NKJV)

"But if a wicked man turns from all his sins which he has committed, keeps all My statutes, and does what is lawful and right, he shall surely live; he shall not die. None of the transgressions which he has committed shall be remembered against him; because of the righteousness which he has done, he shall live." (Ezekiel 18:21-22, NKJV)

Prayer:

Lord, I come to you with all humility and transparency. I open myself to you and I will not hide anything from you. I come to you with boldness and allow you to see me as I am... the good and the bad. Lord I repent of all sin that lives in my mind, body, and soul. I confess that I have committed _____. I acknowledge my sin to you and ask, Will you forgive me for those sins, transgressions, debts, offenses, abominations, and wickedness? Will you forgive me for not being bold to confess your name publicly? Will you forgive me for not using my gifts and talents to glorify your great name? I confess that I haven't been the best (husband, wife, father, mother, brother, sister, employee, etc....) as I can be. I renounce all sin and divorce all ungodly covenants that I have made. Your Word says that if we confess our sins, then you are faithful and just to forgive us and cleanse us from all unrighteousness (1 John 1:9). Holy Spirit search my mind and heart and reveal to me any wrong doings or sin in my life in which I may not be aware of. Show these things to me so that I can acknowledge and confess it, repent from it, and ask for help so that I will gain wisdom and never repeat those offenses. Father, I have faith in your Word and declare boldly that I am forgiven. I accept your blood that you've shed for my freedom from sin. Thank you for releasing me into a new life.

There is no more condemnation now that I have repented and dedicated/rededicated my life to you. Thank you for lifting the penalty of sin from my past and restoring me into everlasting life. The glory belongs to you forever. It is in Jesus' name I pray, amen.

Personal Study/Application:

What do you need to repent from? List 3 scriptures that will help you to not commit that sin again. Try to memorize at least 1 of those scriptures. Meditate on that scripture day and night.

I need to repent from_____

_____

_____

_____

_____

_____

_____

Scripture 1

_____

_____

_____

_____

_____

_____

Scripture 2

_____

_____

_____

_____

_____

_____

_____

Scripture 3

_____

_____

_____

_____

_____

_____

_____

Personal Prayer

_____

_____

_____

_____

_____

_____

_____

Day 1: Repentence

Find the hidden words that are associated with repentance.

```
Q R P E N I T E N C E U O N Q U G F M U
J C A F G C Q S C H S A X W P U U O E D
T O H B W Z D L M O B W X L I G Y R Z G
E N W O S O E I L X X F A L S T R G P Z
S T D A W A R Q L T I M T T N R X I M D
K R E J N T H R L D E P L O R E W V B H
W I M S T F W C O N I G C H A N G E L W
O T E J T X K I T S O N V D M B B N L Y
U I N A A T O N E I Z J E C R R V E E J
W O E W A R D H T I W F W F O K H S F A
X N S T Q H Z L T Y A X G U F B U S K J
B Z R H B S M S Y S A L I Q E P S U W L
A B O W Y C N E R A P S N A R T Y S J O
Q G M B T O J G I C U N E L Z T D H L B
S O E Y Z E R K H K F M Y T S P U J N I
Q S R L L I E K Z J J R J E O C L H T U
S D P A E D E R L O G Y N R R O C U L S
H K A F V V H S F W A O B G J F R G P V
E Y X S F M E J J E H F E E E N N T L G
Y Y B D E Z I G O L O P A R C Q M N A H
```

APOLOGIZE	DEPLORE	HONESTY	REMORSE
ATONE	FORGIVENESS	LAMENT	SORROW
CHANGE	FREE	PENITENCE	TRANSPARENCY
CLEANSE	GRIEF	REFORM	TURN
CONTRITION	GUILT	REGRET	WITHDRAW

The Daniel Way: 21 Days of Fasting and Prayer to Reboot Your Entire Being

Day 2: Purification

Date: _____ /_____/_____

In general, purification is a lot like repentance. It takes honesty and transparency to reveal the sins we've all committed. However, a deeper level of honesty and transparency is required when presenting your entire being unto God. When we repent, oftentimes we confess our sin and pray for guidance not to repeat the same offense. We offer God fruit that is already rotten. How often do we offer God the seed that will produce the rotten fruit? I'm talking about the desire to sin, not just the sin itself. According to Merriam-Webster Dictionary, purification means, *"the act or an instance of purifying or of being purified."* Although the definition is true, the meaning did not match what I saw in the spirit. So, I found the Oxford Living Dictionary and its 3-part definition for purification means, "1) The removal of contaminants from something. 2) The process of extracting something from a substance. 3) The process of making something spiritually or ceremonially clean." Prayerfully these definitions will provide clarity in that God not only wants to deal with your sin, but He also wants to deal with why you want to sin or why the sin is there – not just dealing with dirty water, but more so the cause of why the water is dirty. In the Book of John chapter 13, you will find the story of Jesus washing the disciples' feet. Peter objected the idea of Jesus washing his feet. He was more concerned about hierarchy because Jesus is Lord and in Peter's mind a lord should not operate as a servant. Hear Jesus' response (see verse 8); Jesus said, "If you don't allow me to wash your dirty feet, then you will not be able to spend eternal life with me." Peter sarcastically responded, "Well, don't just wash my feet, but my hands and my head too!" Peter was trying to say that he really wanted to spend eternity with the Lord. But Jesus replied, "You are already clean. It's just your feet (the dirty part of you) that needs attention." The KJV uses the word "whit" which means, "the smallest part imaginable". It is in reference to the part of you that is not so obvious. Believers can be a lot like Peter in the sense that we are willing to offer God parts of us that are already cleansed – the parts of us that we consider usable. We withhold the parts of us that are shameful and dirty even if it goes against our ideology just as Peter's first thought. We must allow God in our entire life (past, present, and future) to clean out these webs in the catted corners of our lives while exposing those things to God that we've kept a secret.

Scripture References:

(see Activity section)

Prayer:

Holy Spirit, I ask that you zoom in on my entire life – my past, my present, and my future. I submit all unclean parts of my being unto you. Oh Lord, purify me from within. Purge me until there is nothing left. Don't leave any spot, wrinkle, or blemish untouched. I give you permission to interrupt anything that is going on behind the scene within me. Wash me clean Oh Lord, even the parts of my mind that hold memories of my past. Don't allow the enemy to bring up past wrongdoings to lure me into temptation again. Purify all residue from which I came out of. Purify me so well that there is no indication nor evidence that will tie my current being to my past sins. Search my heart O God; I am under the scope of you. Transform me into your image – the way you made mankind in the beginning. I will be so careful to praise, honor, and worship your Holy Name forever. In Jesus' name, amen.

Personal Study/Application:

By this time, you may have repented from past sins. I truly thank God for that. Now it's time for you to start confronting the areas in which you may be weak and seek God for divine strategies throughout your process of purification. Please keep in mind that this should happen daily, not just this one day of the fast. On the left side, list at least 5 areas of your life that you feel needs purifying. For example: ungodly habits or addictions, negative mindsets, corrupt communication, resentment, guilt and shame, etc. On the right side, list your desired outcome that corresponds to that area of your life. Lastly, in the middle, list some things you can do that can put you in the position of having the outcome you listed on the right. Think of the middle column as a link between sinner and saint, old and new, dirty and clean, darkness and light, wrong and right... We'll call this The Link of Transformation. It is a way to come to terms with what needs to happen on your end to provoke purification. Pray and seek God for the best strategies for you and your current status.

Areas of Contamination	Link of Transformation	Desired Outcome of Purity
1)_____	_____	_____
_____	_____	_____
_____	_____	_____
_____	_____	_____
2)_____	_____	_____
_____	_____	_____
_____	_____	_____
_____	_____	_____
3)_____	_____	_____
_____	_____	_____
_____	_____	_____
_____	_____	_____
4)_____	_____	_____
_____	_____	_____
_____	_____	_____
_____	_____	_____
5)_____	_____	_____
_____	_____	_____
_____	_____	_____

Day 2: Purification

A number of words have been removed from the scripture and placed in a word bank. Use the words from the word bank to fill in the blanks in the scripture. Write the words in the blanks provided. Challenge yourself and try to complete this without using the hint.

"Therefore, since we have these (1)_____, dear friends, let us (2)_____ ourselves from everything that (3)_____ body and (4)_____, perfecting holiness out of (5)_____ for God."
(**Hint:** 2 Corinthians 7:1, NIV)

"He went on: "What comes out of a person is what (6)_____ them. For it is from within, out of a person's heart, that evil thoughts come-sexual immorality, theft, murder, adultery, (7)_____, malice, deceit, lewdness, envy, slander, arrogance and folly. All these evils come from (8)_____ and defile a person." (**Hint:** Mark 7:20 - 23, NIV)

" For the grace of God has appeared that offers salvation to all people. 12 It teaches us to say "(9)_____" to ungodliness and worldly (10)_____, and to live (11)_____, upright and godly lives in this present age, 13 while we wait for the blessed hope-the appearing of the glory of our great God and Savior, Jesus Christ, 14 who gave himself for us to (12)_____ us from all (13)_____ and to purify for himself a people that are his very own, eager to do what is (14)_____." (**Hint:** Titus 2:11 - 14, NIV)

reverence	inside	contaminates	greed
redeem	promises	purify	good
No	defiles	spirit	self-controlled
passions	wickedness		

Day 3: Sanctification

Date: _____ / _____ / _____

Sanctification is a process that every believer should experience. To sanctify yourself means to purposefully separate yourself from the things of this world so that you will be fit for God's use. There is no step-by-step program or time frame that guarantees you to be successful in this process. For some, it may take a few weeks. For others, it may take a few months. Realistically, it may take a few weeks to rid yourself from impurity in one area of your life and it may take a few months to rid a different impurity in another area of your life. Sanctification cannot be rushed. You must have a relationship with the Holy Spirit so that He can assist you and teach you how to disassociate yourself (mind, body, and soul...mentally, physically, emotionally, and spiritually) from ungodly surroundings and behaviors. Truthfully, you should never leave the process of sanctification as if it is something that you can finish or earn some sort of certification. No matter how long you have been in fellowship with the Lord, sanctifying yourself should be a daily action that you put into place. In other words, sanctification is your responsibility. When you have sanctified yourself, then God will come in and sanctify you. Today we will go to the Father in prayer to seek wisdom for supernatural guidance on how to mortify the deeds of the flesh and separate ourselves from what has become the norm. We will not make room or create any gray areas. We will completely cross over and not settle with being close to the borderline and still say that we are safe. This includes the music we listen to, the entertainment we watch, the conversations we engage in, and any substance that we put into our bodies.

Scripture References:

"Now may the God of peace Himself sanctify you completely; and may your whole spirit, soul, and body be preserved blameless at the coming of our Lord Jesus Christ." (1 Thessalonians 5:23, NKJV)

"Sanctify yourselves therefore, and be ye holy: for I am the Lord your God. And ye shall keep my statutes, and do them: I am the Lord which sanctify you." (Leviticus 20:7-8, KJV)

"And Joshua said to the people, "Sanctify yourselves, for tomorrow the Lord will do wonders among you." (Joshua 3:5, NKJV)

"Do not be unequally yoked together with unbelievers. For what fellowship has righteousness with lawlessness? And what communion has light with darkness? And what accord has Christ with Belial? Or what part has a believer with an unbeliever? And what agreement has the temple of God with idols? For you are the temple of the living God. As God has said: "I will dwell in them and walk among *them.* I will be their God, and they shall be My people. Therefore, come out from among them and be separate, says the Lord. Do not touch what is unclean, and I will receive you. I will be a Father to you, and you shall be My sons and daughters, says the Lord Almighty." (2 Corinthians 6:14-18, NKJV)

Prayer:

Heavenly Father, will you give me the strength to detach myself from all impure thoughts, all relationships that are spiritually unhealthy, all addictions, all forms of lust, and all places that do not bring glory to your name? Holy Spirit, will you reveal to me anything that I should not be in fellowship with? I am on a journey and I do not want to be deceived. Show them to me so that I can let go of them. I became light because you are the Light, and I decree that all darkness in my life and around my life shall be exposed and expelled out of my life. It is in Jesus' name I pray, amen.

Personal Study/Application:

Make a list of people, places, or things that are in your life that you need to separate from. Below each item, write why this person/people, place, or thing is not good for you.

PEOPLE

_____

_____

_____

_____

_____

_____

Why are these people not good for you?

_____

_____

_____

_____

_____

PLACES

_____

_____

_____

_____

_____

Why are these places not good for you?

_____

_____

_____

_____

_____

THINGS

_____

_____

_____

_____

_____

Why are these things not good for you?

_____

_____

_____

_____

_____

_____

NOTE:

You must understand that the reason why these people, places, and things are not good for you is the exact same purpose of the enemy. You must remember that the enemy's job is to kill, steal, and destroy (John 10:10). Christ's job is the opposite of that. His job is to give you life more abundantly. So which result would you rather have? Our Father gives us freedom to decide.

Day 3: Sanctification

Use the New King James Version (NKJV) to complete the crossword puzzle. Look up the scriptures that are listed under the Across and Down sections. Find the "important" word that coincides with today's fasting topic. Then write that word in the crossword puzzle.

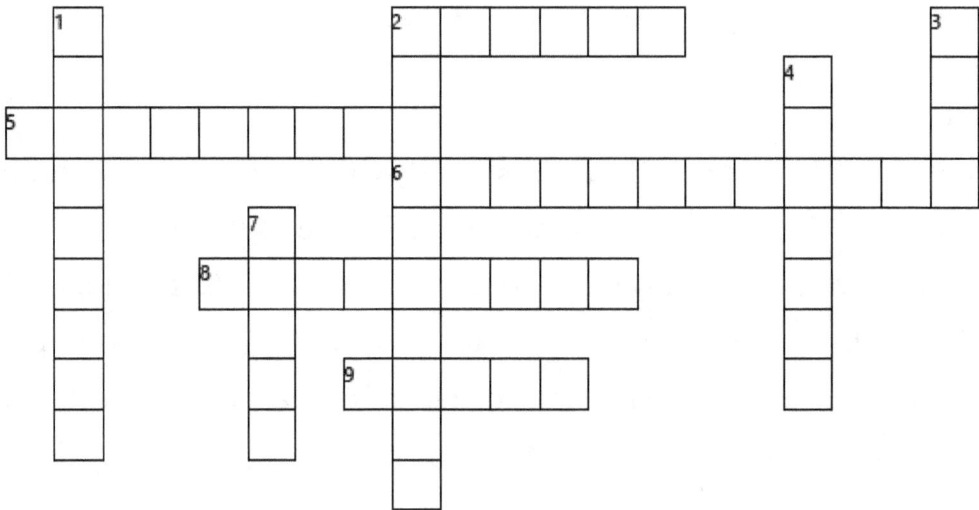

ACROSS

2. Ephesians 1:13

5. 1 Thessalonians 5:23

6. Colossians 2:11

8. Galatians 2:20

9. Acts 26:18

DOWN

2. Ephesians 1:13

5. 1 Thessalonians 5:23

6. Colossians 2:11

8. Galatians 2:20

9. Acts 26:18

Day 4: Adoration & Thanksgiving   Date: _____ /_____/_____

Adoration is something that every Christian should participate in especially when giving thanks. However, I'm not sure if many Christians understand that adoration is perhaps the highest form of worship. Most of today's Christians have adopted a mindset that it doesn't take much to get into the presence of God because after all, "God knows our hearts." I'm sure you've heard that before and possibly confessed that yourself. We must understand that adoration is more than just "Thank you Lord" on our way to work; "Help me Jesus" while looking the mirror; or a whispered hallelujah in church during praise and worship. Adoration is a bit more intense than that. It includes the physical manifestation of your praise and worship while giving thanks to God. It is conducted as a physical expression of worship. In the Bible, it was the Hebrew's custom to prostrate themselves in reverence and respect. (Not only before the Lord but also for people who held authoritative positions.) For example, if you wanted to go to God in prayer to show Him how humble you are and how high He is, then a great way to show this is to bow to your knees while praying or lay flat on the floor with your forehead to the ground while worshiping. Even if you are physically able to manifest your praise and worship in this manner, it can still feel uncomfortable and awkward if you are not use to it. When the Word of God says, "O clap your hands, all ye people; shout unto God with the voice of triumph." (Psalms 47:1, KJV), He really means for you to clap your hands and SHOUT! Not just shout aimlessly, but with a voice of triumph. We have the Victory through Christ! Let's face it; we're comfortable with clapping our hands, but that shouting part... we'd rather not. Essentially there's no difference when we cheer for our favorite team at a ball game. Why can't we use that same physical expression to cheer Jehovah Sabaoth (The Lord of Hosts) when He fights on our behalf? So, spend some time today and for the duration of this fast praising and worshiping God with adoration and thanksgiving. Pay attention to your posture and don't hold back. Meet God in this place and watch Him move on your behalf.

Scripture References:

"At the evening sacrifice I arose from my fasting; and having torn my garment and my robe, I fell on my knees and spread out my hands to the Lord my God." (Ezra 9:5, NKJV)

"Then Abram fell on his face, and God talked with him, saying:" (Genesis 17:3, NKJV)

"He went a little farther and fell on His face, and prayed, saying, "O My Father, if it is possible, let this cup pass from Me; nevertheless, not as I will, but as You *will*." (Matthew 26:39, NKJV)

"And when I saw Him, I fell at His feet as dead. But He laid His right hand on me, saying to me, "Do not be afraid; I am the First and the Last." (Revelation 1:17, NKJV)

"And so it was, when Solomon had finished praying all this prayer and supplication to the LORD, that he arose from before the altar of the LORD, from kneeling on his knees with his hands spread up to heaven." (1 Kings 8:54, NKJV)

"Then King David went in and sat before the LORD; and he said: "Who *am* I, O Lord GOD? And what is my house, that You have brought me this far?" (2 Samuel 7:18, NKJV)

"And she said, "O my lord! As your soul lives, my lord, I am the woman who stood by you here, praying to the Lord." (1 Samuel 1:26, NKJV)

Prayer:

Heavenly Father, I bow before you Oh Lord. I come to you in the humblest way I know how. I lift my hands to you to show you that I surrender to your will and way. I want to show you that I forsake my own will. Whatever you show me God, I'll be sure to obey. I honor you, not because I want something from you, but because you are God and you deserve my praise and worship. Thank you for all the blessings that you have bestowed upon me. I am eternally grateful to you. You have blessed me, covered me, healed me, and delivered me. You are my promise and without you I can't even breathe. It is in you that I live, move, and have my being. You are the source of my strength. Thank you for not giving up on me and continuing to lead me into a righteous path. Thank you for standing up for me and loving me like no one else can. I will continue to give you my life for the rest of my life. It is in Jesus' name I pray, amen.

Personal Study/Application:

What posture did you decide to take to manifest your adoration and thanksgiving? How different was your posture from your normal stance during prayer? Did your new posture have an effect of your prayer? Take the time to journal your experience of praying in a new posture.

_____

_____

_____

_____

_____

_____

_____

_____

_____

_____

_____

_____

_____

_____

_____

_____

_____

_____

Day 4: Adoration & Thanksgiving

The letters of the words below are jumbled. Figure out what the word is and write it on the blank line provided. Listed below are hints in forms of scriptures or definitions. All scriptures are from the New King James Version (NKJV).

1 MACYRRGE _____	11 ITOIETNP _____
2 TBNINIEDECO _____	12 ISAREP _____
3 ITOTYNMES _____	13 ELGEARFNUSST _____
4 ORITEINOGCN _____	14 RCDITE _____
5 DETBSIENSEDN _____	15 EAGCR _____
6 HTAKSN _____	16 TEULNKSSAHNF _____
7 TETIBUR _____	17 DIAGETRTU _____
8 LGIBONATOI _____	18 ANKIHTNSVGGI _____
9 RIECOPAAIPTN _____	19 NTEENLMWDACKOG _____
10 IINVATOCNO _____	20 BISLEGSN _____

1. used to express gratitude or surprise
2. something that promotes goodness or well-being
3. Revelation 12:11
4. special notice or attention
5. something that is owed
6. 1 Thessalonians 5:18
7. 1 Chronicles 18:6
8. 2 Corinthians 9:5
9. a feeling or expression of admiration, approval, or gratitude
10. a calling upon for authority or justification

11. 1 Samuel 1:17
12. Exodus 15:2
13. appreciative of benefits received
14. 1 Peter 2:20
15. Genesis 6:8
16. Acts 24:3
17. the state of being grateful
18. Psalm 100:4
19. 1 Corinthians 16:18
20. Proverbs 10:22

Day 5: My Identity in Christ   Date: _____ /_____/_____

I must admit, this one can be quite challenging for several reasons. One reason is that most Christians know who they are – right now but have no idea who they will become. Others may know who they are to become but have no clue on how to get there or when it will come to pass. Some may identify themselves with their title and some may identify themselves by their gifts and talents. It is difficult to pinpoint who you are in Christ because we are all on a journey and God's plan for our lives will soon unfold as we walk on this Christian journey. Consider this prompt. What if God stripped you from your title, position, gifts and talents, and even your service to others? Really think about this for a moment. What if everything you have ever owned and worked so hard to obtain suddenly was taken away? No title, no position, no gift, no talent, no career, no degree, no pension, no savings account, no stocks and bonds, and no relationships. Now answer this; would you know who you are? Would you know who you are in Christ? I say this because I want you to understand that your titles, positions, gifts and talents, services, degrees, finances, and relationships are not who you are in Christ, but a mere description of what you do in and for the Kingdom of God. Do you want to know who you really are in Christ? You are whomever and whatever the Word of God says you are! This is the point in which you are to cast down all excuses. Forget your past sins, mistakes, intentions, failures, and short comings. You must speak the Word of God through faith concerning your entire being, especially your identity in Him. "But my doctor said…" The Word says that you are healed! "But my bank account is…" The Word says that God is your provider! "But I can't sing like…" The Word says to sing a new song! "But society says..." God said that you are the head and not the tail. You are above and not beneath. And if anyone lays a finger on you, then the Lord himself will repay them for their actions. Don't touch my anointed ones and don't harm my prophets (Psalms 105:15). That, my brothers and sisters, is who you are in Christ, who the Word of God says you are!

Scripture References:

"But God demonstrates His own love toward us, in that while we were still sinners, Christ died for us." (Romans 5:8, NKJV)

"In Him you were also circumcised with the circumcision made without hands, by putting off the body of the sins of the flesh, by the circumcision of Christ," (Colossians 2:11, NKJV)

"who Himself bore our sins in His own body on the tree, that we, having died to sins, might live for righteousness—by whose stripes you were healed." (1 Peter 2:24, NKJV)

Prayer:

Dear God, I desire to be more like you. Will you show me who I am in you? Increase my faith through you Word. Help me to understand that I am who you say that I am. As I continue to walk this Christian journey, I open myself up to you and release my ideology to you. Take out what you need to and rearrange my thinking to match your will for my life. Will you give me the strength to accomplish any task you have set before me? Father,

I am prosperous because you Word says so. I am healed because your Word says so. I am redeemed because your Word says so. No longer will I let my past dictate my destiny. Lord please allow my lifestyle to reflect your Word as you empower me to walk it out and live it out more and more each day. In Jesus' name, amen.

Personal Study/Application:

Look up these verses and consider their meanings carefully. Briefly describe what each scripture says about you. These self-worth Christian affirmations are just the beginning of your journey. Within the pages of the Bible, you will find a vast array of biblical principles and promises that will inspire you as you achieve a stronger self-worth and confidence in living a Christ centered life.

Jeremiah 29:11

_____

_____

_____

_____

_____

Luke 12:6-7

_____

_____

_____

_____

Titus 3:5

_____

_____

_____

_____

_____

Colossians 3:12-14

_____

_____

_____

_____

_____

James 4:6

_____

_____

_____

_____

Romans 12:3

_____

_____

_____

_____

1 John 4:19-21

_____

_____

_____

_____

_____

Matthew 16:26

_____

_____

_____

_____

_____

Philippians 4:8-9

_____

_____

_____

_____

_____

Hebrews 13:5

_____

_____

_____

_____

Day 5: My Identity in Christ

The scripture below has been written in code. Use the hints in the decoder at the top of the page to help IDENTIFY the code (the letters on top are the correct answers, the letters on the bottom are the code, one has been solved for you). Then fill-in the correct letter in the blank space above each code letter in the text. Will you be able to find your "Identity in Christ?"

						T																			
A	B	C	D	E	F	G	H	I	J	K	L	M	N	O	P	Q	R	S	T	U	V	W	X	Y	Z

" ‾   ‾‾‾‾   ‾‾‾‾   ‾‾‾‾‾‾‾   ‾‾‾‾   ‾‾‾‾‾
B   U R F H   T H H Y   V W J V B S B H A   L B G U   V U W B O G ;

‾‾   ‾‾   ‾‾   ‾‾‾‾‾   ‾   ‾‾‾   ‾‾‾‾   ‾‾‾
B G   B O   Y Q   E Q Y N H W   B   L U Q   E B F H ,   T J G

‾‾‾‾‾‾   ‾‾‾‾‾   ‾‾   ‾‾ ;   ‾‾‾   ‾‾‾   ‾‾‾‾
V U W B O G   E B F H O   B Y   P H ;   R Y A   G U H   E B S H

‾‾‾‾‾   ‾   ‾‾‾   ‾‾‾‾   ‾‾   ‾‾‾   ‾‾‾‾   ‾   ‾‾‾‾
L U B V U   B   Y Q L   E B F H   B Y   G U H   S E H O U   B   E B F H

‾‾   ‾‾‾‾‾   ‾‾   ‾‾‾   ‾‾‾   ‾‾   ‾‾‾   ‾‾‾
T X   S R B G U   B Y   G U H   O Q Y   Q S   N Q A ,   L U Q

‾‾‾‾‾   ‾‾   ‾‾‾   ‾‾‾‾   ‾‾‾‾‾‾   ‾‾‾   ‾‾ . "
E Q F H A   P H   R Y A   N R F H   U B P O H S   S Q W   P H . "

‾‾‾‾‾‾‾‾‾   ‾‾‾‾
(N R E R G B R Y O   2 : 2 0 ,   Y K Z F)

Day 6: Purpose for My Life

Like yesterday's fasting focus topic, today's topic can also be as challenging. Everyone has wondered about their life's purpose at some time or another. I find that most people would ponder on this topic at different stages in their life such as a teen, an adult, and at mid-life. Some people may have a set purpose in life. Others may have many purposes as it may change from one season to another. I find that most of the time, your purpose is attached to your unique talents, gifts, and callings. We were created to share those gifts with the world. Consider this fact. There is nobody exactly like you in this entire world nor will there ever be one. And you were chosen to live in this place at this time. Now ask yourself this question. Who can do what you do exactly the way you would do it? No one! Only you can fulfill your purpose and God has given you one life to do it. The responsibility falls on you. You must position yourself to uncover your purpose through your relationship with God. The Father desires to show us His way. We don't even need special abilities. The only ability God requires is availability! So, I can't tell you what your life purpose is. Only God can reveal that to you. However, I can give you a few tips on how to determine what those treasures are that lies within you. Once you discover them, the Lord will show you what to do with them. He will also show you how to use them.

Tips to Help You Find Your Purpose in Life

- First, pray and ask God to reveal His will in your life. He loves to do this...in parts!

- Second, determine the goals or dreams that always seem to find you. This could be part of your destiny. Understand that God is the one who puts His desires in your spirit; so, trust Him.

- Third, watch for direction and guidance. Rarely does God come down from heaven with a lightning bolt and demand your purpose while using a thunderous voice. Instead, He speaks through the everyday world around us. He who has an ear to hear, let them hear.

- Fourth, believe that God has the power, strength, and desire to work in and through your life. His whole point in creating you was so that you could have a close relationship with Him and fulfill your destiny. He created the whole world; don't you think he can handle your life?

Scripture References:

"Jesus said to him, 'You shall love the LORD your God with all your heart, with all your soul, and with all your mind." (Matthew 22:37, NKJV)

"Delight yourself in the Lord and he will give you the desires of your heart." (Psalm 37:4, NKJV)

"I will instruct you and teach you in the way you should go; I will guide you with My eye." (Psalm 32:8, NKJV)

"But you shall receive power when the Holy Spirit has come upon you; and you shall be witnesses to Me in Jerusalem, and in all Judea and Samaria, and to the end of the earth." (Acts 1:8, NKJV)

Prayer:

Father, I humble myself before you to seek your divine direction and will for my life. Lord, will you show me your desire? Show me the paths that you want me to take. I'm asking you to reveal your talents, gifts, and callings that you have placed inside of me. Show me what they are and how to use them for your glory. Reveal the appropriate season and timing in which you would have me to use them and fulfill my purpose. Let me not be afraid, but give me the wisdom, confidence, and the boldness to step out on faith. I trust you and follow you. In Jesus' name, amen.

Personal Study/Application:

On the left column, list some goals or dreams you desire to achieve. In the middle column, list some practical steps to achieve that goal or dream. On the right column, explain how God could get the glory out of that goal or dream.

Goals or Dreams	Practical Steps	God's Glory
1)_____	_____	_____
_____	_____	_____
_____	_____	_____
_____	_____	_____
_____	_____	_____
2)_____	_____	_____
_____	_____	_____
_____	_____	_____
_____	_____	_____
_____	_____	_____
3)_____	_____	_____
_____	_____	_____
_____	_____	_____
_____	_____	_____
_____	_____	_____
4)_____	_____	_____
_____	_____	_____
_____	_____	_____
_____	_____	_____
_____	_____	_____

Day 6: Purpose for My Life

Find the hidden words that are associated with gifts and talents.

```
T U I A H N G F G R R B Z P R A Y E R
Y D G K N Z A N A K O H B D M U S I C
Y B J N M D R Y I I I T E H L V Y H D I
B W M L I C Z P T L T T V C K G S C O Q
Z L G N I T N I A P E H A J I P V H Q U
K Z T X U N I C E C K S R R Z V N B W Z
C O M P U T E R S D J I N O O C R W Z E
V F Q M J P R H W B K B C U L C I E C N
S L L I K S L A C I D E M V O G E S S T
G E I L P D X P K M M Z C P S C N D E R
A X S D B T E A C H I N G H T O K C L E
Q O C A R E G I V E R M Z O K Q A N E P
B V V S Q K Q N O T F F U T B I J O C R
S P E C I A L N E E D S W O R K E R T E
K L K R E Z R T F U A Q X G E T L Z R N
X H W V K M B Q M Z J F I R O F D L I E
N O I T A R T S I N I M D A Z E Q V C U
W V G A R D E N I N G E Z P K P P W I R
Q Y T I L A T I P S O H O H L T V E A B
M T A Z C O O K I N G I B Y S Z I O N X
```

ADMINISTRATION	DECORATING	HOSPITALITY	PRAYER
CAREGIVER	ELECTRICIAN	MEDICAL SKILLS	SERVICE
COMPUTERS	ENTREPRENEUR	MUSIC	SPECIAL NEEDS WORKER
COOKING	FAITH	PAINTING	TEACHING
COUNSELING	GARDENING	PHOTOGRAPHY	WRITING

Day 7: A Sound Mind   Date: _____ / _____ / _____

I am sure you all can relate when I speak of "various aspects of life." When you play various roles, it can be hard to divide yourself while keeping purpose in mind. When you become one person to someone and someone else to another, it can be catastrophic if it's not managed well. For example, I am a husband, father, employee, pastor, business owner, student, brother, uncle, and friend. My responsibilities as a husband are different from my responsibilities as a pastor. My responsibilities as an employee are different from my responsibilities as a business owner. I admit it! There are times when all these responsibilities flood me at once. I foolishly asked God to create another me or create another day in the week. God didn't pay me any mind on that request. However, when I became frustrated with my frustrations, I sincerely prayed to God and asked Him for divine strategies on how to keep everything afloat. Do you know what He did? He sent me leaders who love God and they helped me keep the church balanced. I try my best to honor and thank all leaders for their service to God. Indeed, it is their service but it's also my prayer being answered. Without them, my stress level would be at an all-time high.

Stress is one of the main factors in opposition to having a sound mind. At times it can seem like there's so much to do with so little time. Appointments, meetings, deadlines... you name it! Physical stress, emotional stress, mental stress (however you want to categorize it), can weigh in on your peace of mind.

Additionally, stress is not the only factor that causes an unsound mind. There is so much negativity being advertised in the media that it can cause you to think negatively or conjure up negative emotions that you begin to act negative if left unchecked. The politics, news, killings, devastations, terrorist attacks, etc.... are all presented to you so that you can be "informed". God desires for you to have a sound, peaceful, and sober mind. So, let's fast from all negativity and all forms of stress. Focus on having a sound mind in the Lord. Please be wise and know that because you've decided to focus on having a sound mind today, you will soon be confronted or tempted by all kinds of things that will challenge your peace of mind. Stay in prayer! Don't allow the issues of life deter you from the peace of God.

Scripture References:

"Casting down imaginations, and every high thing that exalteth itself against the knowledge of God, and bringing into captivity every thought to the obedience of Christ;" (2 Corinthians 10:5, KJV)

"You are of God, little children, and have overcome them, because He who is in you is greater than he who is in the world." (1 John 4:4, NKJV)

"For God has not given us a spirit of fear, but of power and of love and of a sound mind." (2 Timothy 1:7, NKJV)

"Finally, brethren, whatever things are true, whatever things *are* noble, whatever things *are* just, whatever things *are* pure, whatever things *are* lovely, whatever things *are* of good report, if *there is* any virtue and if *there is* anything praiseworthy—meditate on these things." (Philippians 4:8, NKJV)

Prayer:

Heavenly Father, thank you for protecting my mind against negative thinking, unstable thoughts, double mindedness, fear, and doubt. Help me oh Lord to stand my ground in you when the enemy comes with his devices. Satan, you are a liar and I will not receive or believe your lies in the Name of Jesus. The Word of God says that greater is He that is in me than he that is in the world. So, I command you to bow to the Christ who lives in me and leave me in Jesus' name. I refuse to give in to fear. I fear the Lord only and He gives me the spirit of power, love and a sound mind! Lord, I thank you for truth, nobility, righteousness, purity, love, and peace. It is in Jesus' name that I pray, receive, and keep my peace this day and every day! Amen!

Personal Study/Application:

What are some things that you have been exposed to that caused you to wavier in your mind? I encourage you to write them down. When you are finished, pray concerning these things and settle this frustration or stress in prayer. When you finish praying, resist the temptation to worry about them or allow stress and negativity to re-enter. Whenever these issues try to rise up, combat them with the instructions of Philippians 4:8 on the previous page.

Day 7: A Sound Mind

Below the blank puzzle grid is a list of positive words that promote a sound mind. Place the words in the correct place on the grid. Tip: Start with letter sizes that have the fewest words. So if there are only 2 words with 7 letters and 5 words with 4 letters, try placing the 7 letter words first.

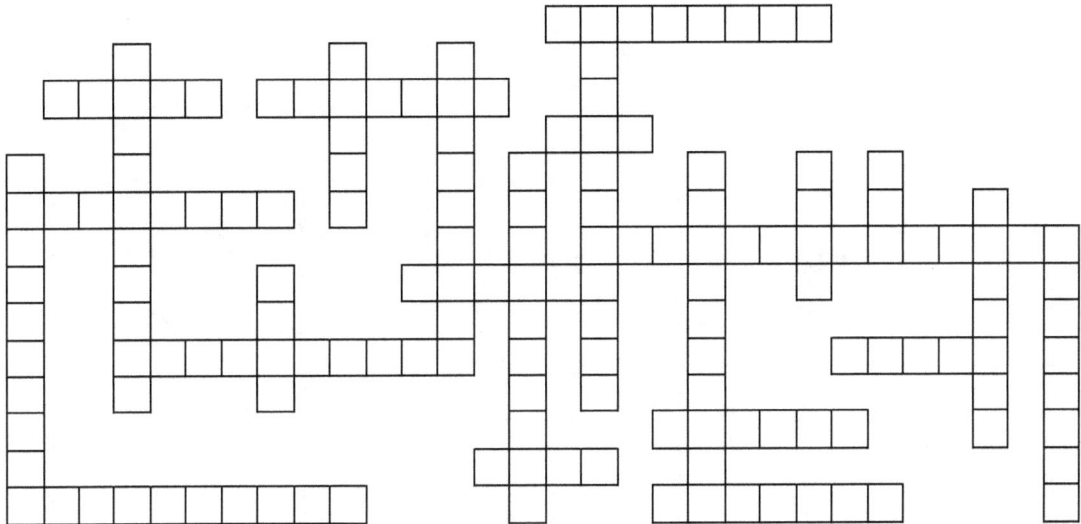

3 Letters	5 Letters	7 Letters	9 Letters	11 Letters
joy	favor	zealous	nurturing	encouraging
yes	whole	healing		
	quiet	believe	10 Letters	14 Letters
4 Letters			productive	accomplishment
calm	6 Letters	8 Letters	unwavering	
kind	giving	truthful	optimistic	
love	divine	restored	victorious	
		innovate	miraculous	
			supportive	

Week 2:

Transforming into the Image of Christ

Day 8: Submission to God   Date: _____ /_____/_____

Let's face it. Some people don't like the word *submission*. To some, that word may bring a negative connotation or maybe a feeling of low self-worth. Others may view it as a form of restriction because who or what they submit to may not agree with their own will. It can become a conflict and cause you to be stubborn and stubbornness is always connected to pride.

Submission, however, has great rewards and it is beneficial to your character. It allows you to release the spirit of pride and enter a covering of protection that comes from God, that is if you are TRULY submitting to God. It can also relieve you from the stress of trying to keep it all together. Everybody has their own story and we all came to Christ differently needing Him to work some things out of us. For Christ to rearrange our lives, we must submit to Him so that He can train us and make us useful for His glory.

Peter is a perfect example of the Lord's training. Without going into much detail, one of Peter's issues involved his confidence in his own natural strength. Jesus had to break his mentality while Peter learned through his own failures. Most of us know the story when Peter was rebuked by Jesus. Although he was looking out for the Lord's best interest, it was not the will of God. The important lesson here is that we must be obedient to God even if it does not make sense to us. Like most of us, Peter had to learn not to place confidence in himself but trust the will of God. You cannot submit to anything you don't trust! A major turning point in Peter's life was after he publicly denied Jesus three times. He was devastated to realize that what the Lord said he would do, he ended up doing. Peter boldly declared he would not deny the Son of God. In his own strength, he did exactly that! However, in that failure, he learned his confidence in himself was NOT enough. I'm sure he had learned to trust the Lord then.

It takes humility to acknowledge that your strongest points are in fact your weakest. We cannot do anything without Christ. If we don't learn this lesson, then how valuable will we be for the kingdom of God? Such people who will not humble themselves are a liability to the Kingdom and can cause more harm than good.

Let's take this time to submit to God's will. Make an effort to submit in every area. Ensure that you are truly submitted even in the areas of your life that you think you are okay in. You'll be surprised to find out how you could be so wrong, when you thought you were so right. Submission to God will teach you a lot about God, yourself, and others. Trust God! Do your best to obey Him even when it does not make sense to you. Have faith in Him and His power, not your own. Listen for Him to speak to you about the areas He need you to submit to Him.

Scripture References:

"I beseech you therefore, brethren, by the mercies of God, that you present your bodies a living sacrifice, holy, acceptable to God, *which is* your reasonable service. And do not be conformed to this world, but be transformed by the renewing of your mind, that you may prove what *is* that good and acceptable and perfect will of God." (Romans 12:1–2, NKJV)

"Then He said to *them* all, "If anyone desires to come after Me, let him deny himself, and take up his cross daily, and follow Me." (Luke 9:23, NKJV)

Prayer:

Heavenly Father, you are the Most High God, you rule and reign forever and ever. I confess that I have my own dreams and goals. But your will means more to me than my own. So please forgive me for making my will to be much more than your will. I submit my entire being to your will and to your way. No longer will I live in the way that I want to live. Teach me your ways so that I can obey you. Cause my ear to hear when you speak. Speak in such a way that I can understand. Increase my faith so that I can release my own strength. Train me oh God, so that I can be fit to be useful as you see fit. I trust that you will complete the work that you started in me. It is in Jesus' name I pray, amen.

Personal Study/Application:

What are some areas in your life that proves you are submitted to God? What are some areas in your life that need improving so that you can show your submission to God? Treat this application as your own personal prayer to help you submit to God.

_____

_____

_____

_____

_____

_____

Day 8: Submission to God

The letters of the words below are jumbled. Figure out what the word is and write it on the blank line provided. Listed below are hints in the form of scriptures or definitions. All scriptures are from the New King James Version (NKJV).

1 SUSIISVBME _____

2 ULER _____

3 NEPAOTDIP _____

4 FAER _____

5 EIHRLTAY _____

6 LIWL _____

7 SETT _____

8 DEDA _____

9 BUITSM _____

10 OSNILWLES _____

11 APEDYR _____

12 ICDNBEOEE _____

13 BEULHM _____

14 UHEAOTTIIRS _____

15 JSECBUT _____

16 AEEPC _____

1. Hebrews 13:17
2. Genesis 3:16
3. Romans 13:1
4. Ephesians 5:21
5. Colossians 3:23
6. Luke 22:42
7. Jeremiah 17:10
8. Romans 7:4

9. James 4:7
10. Philippians 2:3
11. Matthew 26:39
12. Hebrews 5:8
13. 1 Peter 5:6
14. Titus 3:1
15. Romans 8:7
16. Job 22:21

Day 9: Being Filled with the Holy Spirit   Date: _____ /_____/_____

When a sinner becomes a Christian, everything about their life becomes old, and everything about their life becomes new. They are now born again. They have everlasting life. They are now sealed by the Blood of Jesus and by the Holy Spirit. However, this does not mean that all Christians are on the same level or have the same degree of wisdom. The Bible makes a clear distinction between Christians who are spiritual and other Christians who are worldly. (Compare 1 Corinthians 1:2 and 1 Corinthians 3:1) The difference here is that the work of the Holy Spirit is in the heart of a person. Every Christian has access to the Holy Spirit, but not all Christians yield to the direction and instruction of the Holy Spirit. It is important to have the mind of Christ and a heart to obey Him.

To be filled with the Holy Spirit is not dependent on time, but it depends on your level of maturity. This means that it's possible for a new Christian to be filled with the Holy Spirit. In the Old Testament, the Holy Spirit was not regularly revealed. When He was, it was for an assignment that the Lord put on a person. This could have been for wisdom, for skills, or for strength. In the New Testament, the Holy Spirit is in you, not just on you. There is a big difference. All Christians are equally saved, but not all Christians are equally filled with the Holy Spirit. When a Christian sin, the Holy Spirit becomes grieved. This will affect our capacity to be filled. Therefore, it is imperative that we live a holy life. If we stay in the Spirit, then we will not fulfill the lust of the flesh. If we stay in the Spirit, then we will be able to walk in the Spirit. Now walking in the Spirit does not mean that you are speaking in tongues all day. It means that you are living a holy life in every area of your life. It also does not mean you will never sin again. It does mean that the power of sin over your life becomes less and less as the power of God within you to walk in the Spirit becomes greater and greater. This spirit-filled life makes the Word of God confirm its power and authority. It gives you the power to confront the enemy without fear because you know that the enemy seeks to destroy us. So, follow God's Word at all cost. Stay alive and sanctified. He promises to keep you filled!

Scripture References:

"And do not be drunk with wine, in which is dissipation; but be filled with the Spirit," (Ephesians 5:1, NKJV)

"I say then: Walk in the Spirit, and you shall not fulfill the lust of the flesh." (Galatians 5:16, NKJV)

"If we live in the Spirit, let us also walk in the Spirit." (Galatians 5:25, NKJV)

Prayer:

Heavenly Father, you are the Potter and I am the clay. Continue to shape me and mold me according to how you see fit. Then fill me up and allow me to overflow with your Spirit. Let it boil over like never before. You are my Oil that never runs out. Holy Spirit, you are my Teacher, so teach me the ways of the Lord. I submit to your ways. In Jesus' name, amen.

Personal Study/Application:

Find some more scriptures in the Bible that pertains to the Holy Spirit. Conduct your own Bible Study about being filled with the Holy Spirit. Determine what God will have you to do to continue to make more room for the Holy Spirit to operate in your daily life.

_____

_____

_____

_____

_____

_____

_____

_____

_____

_____

_____

_____

_____

_____

_____

_____

_____

Day 9: Filled with the Holy Spirit

The scripture below has been written in code. Use the hints in the decoder at the top of the page to help identify the code (the letters on top are the correct answers, the letters on the bottom are the code, one has been solved for you). Then fill-in the correct letter in the blank space above each code letter in the text. Can you find out what happens when you are filled with the Holy Spirit?

	H																									
A	B	C	D	E	F	G	H	I	J	K	L	M	N	O	P	Q	R	S	T	U	V	W	X	Y	Z

ABZK VBZ INX SM EZKVZFSHV BNI MQDDX

FSCZ, VBZX AZWZ NDD ATVB SKZ NFFSWI

TK SKZ EDNFZ. NKI HQIIZKDX VBZWZ

FNCZ N HSQKI MWSC BZNRZK, NH SM N

WQHBTKP CTPBVX ATKI, NKI TV MTDDZI

VBZ ABSDZ BSQHZ ABZWZ VBZX AZWZ

HTVVTKP. VBZK VBZWZ NEEZNWZI VS

VBZC ITRTIZI VSKPQZH, NH SM MTWZ, NKI

SKZ HNV QESK ZNFB SM VBZC. NKI VBZX

AZWZ NDD MTDDZI ATVB VBZ BSDX

HETWTV NKI UZPNK VS HEZNL ATVB SVBZW

VSKPQZH, NH VBZ HETWTV PNRZ VBZC

QVVZWNKFZ. (NFVH 2:1-4, KLYR)

Day 10: Growth in Christ   Date: _____ /_____/_____

Everybody has a story about how their life was when they were growing up. Most would agree that the changes you experienced during that time were often difficult with so much uncertainty. We all reach maturity at different times. Some people reach it quicker than others. Well, growing up in your spiritual life can be just as challenging. Similarly, to our natural life, some people reach spiritual maturity quicker than others. When we conversate with other Christians, it is important not to assume their level of spiritual maturity. You'll be surprised how well their book is written, when your thinking was contrary to their cover. I've been in ministry for years and I can honestly say that the opposite of that statement is also true. I've seen people with beautiful covers, but when I started to read their "book", it had many errors. Therefore, we should always call on the Chief Editor, Jesus Christ who is the author and finisher of our faith. What He has begun, He will complete it in you. Trusting Him is required.

As we continue this Christian journey, there will come a time where we need to move past the elementary teachings of righteousness. If we concentrate only on the basic foundations of truth, we can become stagnate which may prevent us from growing in Christ and learning about the deeper truths of the Word. For example, Isaac Newton said, "What goes up, must come down." I'm sure you've heard that before. This was Newton's way to describe the Law of Gravity. This is an elementary truth. However, there is another law in which I like to describe as, "What goes up, doesn't necessarily mean that it has to come down, right now!" This is where the Law of Aerodynamics comes into play. Consider an airplane when it flies. During its flight, the foundational law is now challenged because another law is in effect. Paul explained it best when he stated that he had a heart to love and serve God, but he found another law warring in his members, which was the law of sin. His conflict (and many of ours) was that he realized that both laws were working at the same time. This led him to find Jesus, the Law of Grace, to challenge and defy the other law at work with in him.

This was how the Word of God was written. The basics of our faith was the law of God written in the Old Testament. Then Jesus came and built on top of that, never claiming the first law to be false. In fact, He said that the law was holy and just. He became the fulfillment of the law and introduced the Law of Grace. So, let's go deeper in God. Don't allow yourself to be satisfied with the basics of Christianity but pray for deeper levels of truth so that you can grow in your relationship with the Father. You don't have to leave the basics as they are always there to guide you. The "basics" are the rules and regulations. As you're growing in God, your relationship becomes much more than rules and regulations. Build on top of the basics and live life accordingly.

Scripture Reference:
"...of whom we have much to say, and hard to explain, since you have become dull of hearing. For though by this time you ought to be teachers, you need *someone* to teach you again the first principles of the oracles of God; and you have come to need milk and not solid food. For everyone

who partakes *only* of milk *is* unskilled in the word of righteousness, for he is a babe. But solid food belongs to those who are of full age, *that is,* those who by reason of use have their senses exercised to discern both good and evil. Therefore, leaving the discussion of the elementary *principles* of Christ, let us go on to perfection, not laying again the foundation of repentance from dead works and of faith toward God, of the doctrine of baptisms, of laying on of hands, of resurrection of the dead, and of eternal judgment. And this we will do if God permits. (Hebrews 5:11-6:3, NKJV)

Prayer:

Father God in the name of Jesus, I praise and honor your holy name. Lord, I have a great desire to know you more and to please you. I want to have a greater love for you and to show you my commitment. Grace me Oh God so that I may dwell in your presence. Holy Spirit, teach me the ways of the Lord so that I can honor Him in all my being. Cause me to grow in you. Raise me up to maturity. Give me the mindset and desire to learn more of your Word so that I may apply it to my life. Cause me to develop, grow, and mature that each year I am growing more and more – not stagnant and not stunted. Don't let me grow older without growing wiser in the things of God. Train me in your ways so that I can receive deeper levels of truth. I trust that you will lead me every step of the way. In Jesus' name, amen.

Personal Study/Application:

Imagine yourself at the place in God in which you desire to be. Think of the person who you desire to be in God. From that place, your future you, write a letter to yourself now. What would your future you say to your current you?

_____

_____

_____

_____

_____

_____

_____

_____

_____

_____

_____

_____

_____

_____

_____

_____

_____

_____

_____

_____

_____

_____

_____

_____

_____

_____

_____

_____

What do you think you would need to do in order to be your future you?

_____

_____

_____

_____

_____

_____

_____

_____

Day 10: Growth in Christ

A number of words have been removed from the scripture and placed in a word bank. Use the words from the word bank to fill in the blanks in the scripture. Write the words in the blanks provided. Challenge yourself and try to complete this without using the hint.

"Therefore, laying aside all malice, all deceit, (1)_____, envy, and all evil speaking, as newborn babes, desire the pure (2)_____ of the word, that you may (3)_____ thereby, if indeed you have tasted that the Lord is gracious. Coming to Him as to a living stone, rejected indeed by men, but chosen by God and precious, you also, as living stones, are being (4)_____ (5)_____ a spiritual house, a holy priesthood, to offer up spiritual (6)_____ acceptable to God through Jesus Christ." (**Hint:** 1 Peter 2:1-5, NKJV)

"For this reason we also, since the day we heard it, do not cease to pray for you, and to ask that you may be filled with the (7)_____ of His will in all wisdom and spiritual (8)_____; that you may walk worthy of the Lord, fully pleasing Him, being (9)_____ in every good work and (10)_____ in the (11)_____ of God;" (**Hint:** Colossians 1:9-10, NKJV)

"But when that which is (12)_____ has come, then that which is in part will be done (13)_____. When I was a (14)_____, I spoke as a child, I understood as a child, I thought as a child; but when I became a man, I put away (15)_____ things. For now we see in a mirror, dimly, but then face to face. Now I know in (16)_____, but then I shall know just as I also am known." (**Hint:** 1 Corinthians 13:10-12, NKJV)

up	milk	away	increasing
perfect	knowledge	part	grow
fruitful	sacrifices	hypocrisy	knowledge
built	child	understanding	childish

Day 11: Protecting Your Gates

Date: _____ /_____/_____

As Kingdom citizens, we are to be careful of how we engage worldly systems. We are in the world but not of the world. The world's system has an agenda to program and desensitize us from righteous living. This agenda has crept into the media, affected the laws, and penetrated the schools. Their agenda is now of the norm (from a worldly perspective). They used to advertise such things subliminally, but now, it's out there loud and proud. Is it necessary for a half-naked woman in a G-string to advertise dental floss? Or do they think they are funny by collating the G-string and the dental floss? Messages like this are broadcasted everywhere. It happens so much that society doesn't have a personal judgement about it because now it's normal to see such things. Must they advertise alcohol with the next big game? Must they broadcast movies and shows with a plot that focuses on adultery and the pleasures of sin? We don't have to seek for such displays (not that we would want to...hopefully) because it is right there in front of our face each day. So, what are we supposed to do about it? We have the responsibility to keep our souls pure before God despite what the world has to offer. The best way to do this is to protect our gates.

These gates are our senses. In other words, we must monitor what we hear, see, feel or touch, taste, and smell. If you are not rooted and grounded in the Word, the pleasures of sin can overtake you. "Pleasures" is what the world thinks it is; we know better! You know what sin you liked in the past or still have an appetite for. Let's agree that that needs to be destroyed. Be honest with yourself. If you allow room for it, even a little bit, you could be drawn away from the mind of Christ and be tempted to fulfill the lust of your flesh.

Make a conscious effort today to monitor those things that try to enter your gates without your permission. Stop allowing things into your life that you already know are harmful. Don't look at, listen to, taste, or touch anything that does not give God glory. This will be a challenge because evil is all around us. Paul said that when I would do good, evil is present. (Romans 7:21).

Scripture References:

"The lamp of the body is the eye. If therefore your eye is good, your whole body will be full of light. But if your eye is bad, your whole body will be full of darkness. If therefore the light that is in you is darkness, how great *is* that darkness!" (Matthew 6:22-23, NKJV)

"Keep your heart with all diligence, for out of it *spring* the issues of life." (Proverbs 4:23, NKJV)

"If your right eye causes you to sin, pluck it out and cast it from you; for it is more profitable for you that one of your members perish, than for your whole body to be cast into hell. And if your right hand causes you to sin, cut it off and cast it from you; for it is more profitable for you that one of your members perish, than for your whole body to be cast into hell." (Matthew 5:29-30 NKJV)

"No temptation has overtaken you except such as is common to man; but God is faithful, who will not allow you to be tempted beyond what you are able, but with the temptation will also make the way of escape, that you may be able to bear it." (1 Corinthians 10:13, NKJV)

Prayer:

Holy Spirit, endow me with your anointing and fill me up with your power so that I can have the authority to reject anything that pleases my flesh. Arrest me if you see me yielding to temptation. Deliver me from the powers of darkness and not just the darkness itself. Destroy every desire within me that is not like God. I reject the world's systems and what it has to offer. I close my eyes to lust and will not take a second look. Cover my ears from the chatter of gossip and other worldly chatter. Allow me to only hear your voice Oh Lord and your direction. Keep me safe as I run to the Strong Tower. Cause me to be numb to the devices of the enemy. Let your light shine through me so that others can see You. I seal this prayer with the Blood of Jesus, and in Jesus' name I pray, amen.

Personal Study/Application:

What are some things you noticed today that you saw, heard, smelt or felt that wasn't of God? What did you do to counter act what you perceived?

_____

_____

_____

_____

_____

Day 11: Protecting Your Gates

Here are some words in which you are highly encouraged to protect your gates from. The letters of the words below are jumbled. Figure out what the word is and write it on the blank line provided. Listed below are hints in forms of definitions or descriptions.

1 TUSL _____

2 ALCCUSUMSERI _____

3 GRDEE _____

4 HERTAD _____

5 CHESATINGLAEF _____

6 SUTERRECHPCOP _____

7 TJERSE _____

8 LOTUYNTG _____

9 REAF _____

10 SSPGIO _____

11 ARDMA _____

12 TPIRAYFON _____

13 FTRSIE _____

14 DSALERN _____

15 VEYN _____

16 NGREA _____

17 RCFINOOAINT _____

18 TDALRUYE _____

1. sexual desire
2. Songs that do not glorify God
3. selfish desires
4. intense dislike or ill will
5. lies wrapped in truth
6. putrid or disgusting words to the recipient (2 words)
7. a person who habitually plays the fool
8. overeating
9. frightened or worried
10. he say, she say
11. conflicting stories or situations
12. curses
13. angry or bitter disagreement over fundamental issues
14. a false spoken statement damaging to a person's reputation
15. a feeling of discontented or resentful longing aroused by someone else's possessions
16. having a strong feeling of or showing annoyance, displeasure, or hostility
17. sex without covenant
18. infidelity

Day 12: Strengthen Your Prayer Life   Date: _____ /_____/_____

Many years ago, I attended a Praise and Worship seminar at my local church. We started talking about prayer and how we can use it as a weapon against the enemy. The instructor asked a question, "Should Christians pray loud or should they pray softly?" My answer was, "It depends on your relationship with God." A young minister (young in ministry, not in age) had a lot to say about my answer to the instructor's question. This young minister hounded me as if I just blasphemed God. She went on-and-on about how I was so wrong to say that. She began to explain that everybody doesn't pray the same way and that I should not judge a person's prayer life based on the volume of their prayer. I mean she went in on me! So, I had to clarify because everything she said was based on assumptions. I began to explain that the reason I said, "It depends on their relationship with God" is because I literally meant that it depends on your relationship with God! Some people may pray loudly because they feel close to God. Others may pray loudly because they may feel far from God and may elevate their voice to a shout so that they may reach Him. On the contrary, some may pray softly because they feel as though God is right there and they begin to whisper directly into His ears. She assumed that I was trying to say that people who pray softly are not as close to God as those who pray loudly. That never came out of my mouth. Praying loudly does not strengthen your prayer life, although it could strengthen your confidence.

To strengthen your prayer life is to pray with authority by using the Word of God as your base. You can strengthen your prayer life when you learn that there are several types of prayers. For example, your prayer can be for your enemy or against your enemy. Your prayer can be asking God for help or establish a decree in your prayer by telling the devil to stand down. There are prayers of repentance, grace, warfare, mercy, forgiveness, blessings, provision, wisdom, direction etc. To strengthen your prayer life means to go deeper in prayer. It is time to change your prayers from the usual prayers that you pray before meals and before bed. To help you get stronger in your prayer life, I suggest for you to pray in detail; be specific. For example, a basic prayer would sound like, "Lord, bless my family." A more detailed prayer would consist of calling every family member out by name. Start with one family member, and pray specific details about that person such as their salvation, their deliverance, their mind, their marriage, their goals, their finances, their lifestyle, etc. Don't hold back. When you are finished with that family member, go on to the next family member and pray details about them. Not only will you begin to flow in prayer, but you will also spend more time in prayer. If you don't know what to say, then you can always read the Word of God as a base for your prayers. The Lord loves to be reminded of His Word. You will increase your faith as you pray and hear the Word.

What if this was your last day on earth and you were only allowed to pray one time for that day. How would you pray? Would your prayer be any different than how you would normally pray? Remember that the Holy Spirit is there to help you pray. He can give you words to say as well. Prayer is the direct connection to God to communicate your deepest thoughts and needs. So, when you pray, pray as if you are praying that once in a lifetime prayer.

Scripture References:

"Now this is the confidence that we have in Him, that if we ask anything according to His will, He hears us." (1 John 5:14, NKJV)

"And may You hear the supplications of Your servant and of Your people Israel, when they pray toward this place. Hear from heaven Your dwelling place, and when You hear, forgive." (2 Chronicles 6:21, NKJV)

"Watch and pray, lest you enter into temptation. The spirit indeed is willing, but the flesh is weak." (Matthew 26:41, NKJV)
"The Lord is near to all who call upon Him, to all who call upon Him in truth." (Psalm 145:18, NKJV)

Prayer:

Instead of giving you a prayer today, I want you to spend time to strengthen your own prayers. More info will be given in the Personal Study/Application section.

Personal Study/Application:

Make a list of things that you want to pray about or people who you would like to pray for. Practice spending time in prayer concerning these things or people. Make sure to pray in detail about each thing or person. Be specific. Remember to refer to the scriptures as a guide to help you pray.

Day 12: Strengthen Your Prayer Life

In the word bank are kingdom terms that you can use in prayer. Can you find these powerful words?

```
B  I  N  D  N  X  L  E  J  W  I  E  X  L  L  O  O  S  E  Q
C  Q  A  G  V  O  U  K  N  T  M  X  Q  L  N  G  M  R  T  P
G  J  C  T  Z  Q  E  I  B  J  O  O  R  N  S  W  A  X  A  Y
W  L  I  F  Q  A  R  N  Q  J  P  A  H  A  R  C  V  J  G  Q
P  R  E  C  N  I  R  G  K  B  U  U  E  F  Z  C  I  Y  I  F
U  K  P  G  H  Q  I  D  J  P  J  T  L  C  P  D  C  B  V  X
A  S  M  E  I  A  Y  O  A  U  N  H  O  H  L  O  T  G  A  K
M  U  S  O  K  S  J  M  M  P  B  O  U  T  H  O  O  F  N  C
S  S  C  G  B  J  L  E  T  M  T  R  D  U  E  L  R  C  A  E
Z  H  X  A  A  E  C  A  Y  D  O  I  I  S  E  B  Y  N  O  F
R  K  I  L  R  R  L  S  T  S  X  T  V  B  R  S  K  I  T  G
C  C  U  F  R  F  Z  B  X  E  M  Y  I  O  C  T  K  F  E  N
S  A  P  U  T  O  O  F  G  Z  E  J  N  V  E  R  S  W  V  S
T  I  R  V  B  R  J  R  E  V  E  S  E  E  D  A  J  H  G  Y
M  S  O  C  T  C  E  C  Z  H  D  M  U  R  B  T  U  L  X  S
Q  W  O  O  X  E  M  D  M  Y  X  B  P  R  L  E  C  N  A  C
K  K  T  S  I  S  J  E  E  Z  O  C  D  U  Y  G  P  G  I  B
L  G  Z  M  W  R  O  R  B  E  G  W  Q  L  E  I  F  M  X  U
I  A  L  O  C  J  S  Q  X  Y  M  N  G  E  Z  E  R  N  I  L
I  V  L  S  G  M  B  G  M  Y  I  D  M  T  A  S  U  B  F  I
```

AUTHORITY	BIND	BLOOD	CANCEL
COSMOS	DECREE	DIVINE	FORCES
KINGDOM	LEGISLATE	LOOSE	NAVIGATE
OVERRULE	REDEEM	SEVER	SHIFT

The Daniel Way: 21 Days of Fasting and Prayer to Reboot Your Entire Being

Day 13: Greater Wisdom   Date: _____ /_____/_____

I'm not going to ask you to call yourself out...just yet. But I'm sure you can relate to this one. Somewhere in your journey, I know you have done something foolish. So have I...many times! It doesn't matter if you are a man or a woman; saved or not saved; young or old, you have found yourself in this category at some time or another. It could have been a mistake, or it could have been intentional. In any case, my prayer is that we learn from our foolish ways.

To learn from those errors, you must ask God for wisdom. The Bible says, "If any of you lacks wisdom, let him ask of God, who gives to all liberally and without reproach, and it will be given to him." (James 1:5, NKJV) I truly believe that if you ask God for wisdom, He will freely give it to you. And when you need more wisdom, He will give you more. You need wisdom. The enemy is very cunning, and sometimes (if you're not careful) he can outwit you. When you ask God for greater wisdom, He will give you divine strategies to fit your needs. For example, if you were at a crossroads in your life and you didn't know whether to turn left or right, just ask God for greater wisdom. He will give you direction. He will either tell you to turn left, turn right, don't move, or back up and get out of there as fast as you can! Sometimes, to let the truth be told, we should have taken a right turn a mile ago, and that's why we ended up at the crossroads. Am I talking right? I am a witness that the Holy Spirit operates like that. I've been there and have done that. I've learned not to move until He tells me to.

King Solomon was the wisest man known to live, besides Jesus of course. Jesus' wisdom came directly from the Father. Now that you have God's wisdom living in you, don't you think that you can be as wise, if not more than Solomon? To God be the glory and I thank Jesus Christ for what He has done. He has made this great level of wisdom available to you. You can use it on your job or career, finances, education, family, and ministry. The work of the Holy Spirit is endless. So, how could you ever be confused when you have access to the Source of all wisdom living inside of you? Tap into the wisdom of God for your life, today!

Scripture References:

"... that the God of our Lord Jesus Christ, the Father of glory, may give to you the spirit of wisdom and revelation in the knowledge of Him," (Ephesians 1:17, NKJV)

"However, we speak wisdom among those who are mature, yet not the wisdom of this age, nor of the rulers of this age, who are coming to nothing. But we speak the wisdom of God in a mystery, the hidden *wisdom* which God ordained before the ages for our glory," (1 Corinthians 2:6-7, NKJV)

Prayer:

Father, I seek your wisdom and truth. Will you give me greater wisdom so that I can have the power to make sound decisions? Will you give me a level of wisdom that will prevent me from being entangled in the enemy's snare? Will you grace me with a level of wisdom that increases the gift of discerning of spirits, so that I can distinguish good from evil. Bless me with a level of wisdom that will warn me to put up my shield when the enemy has thrown his fiery darts. Wake me up oh God before I enter deception. Allow me to use your wisdom concerning my finances and my journey. Endow me with wisdom so that I can be a better spouse, a better parent, a better employee, a better boss, and a better friend. Let your wisdom live in me, now and forever. In Jesus' name, amen.

Personal Study/Application:

What areas in your life do you lack wisdom? Write them down and pray about each one. Then seek the Lord in His Word for the wisdom you need or seek out godly counsel in the areas you need wisdom. If you don't know, then ask God to reveal your lack of wisdom, then pray accordingly.

_____

_____

_____

_____

_____

_____

_____

_____

_____

_____

_____

_____

_____

Day 13: Greater Wisdom

A number of words have been removed from the scripture and placed in a word bank. Use the words from the word bank to fill in the blanks in the scripture. Write the words in the blanks provided. Challenge yourself and try to complete this without using the hint. (Hint: Colossians 2:2-32, NKJV)

"that their (1)_____ may be (2)_____, being knit together in

(3)_____, and (4)_____ to all (5)_____ of the full

assurance of (6)_____, to the knowledge of the (7)_____ of

God, both of the (8)_____ and of (9)_____, in whom are

(10)_____ all the treasures of (11)_____ and

(12)_____. "

Christ	mystery	understanding	knowledge	encouraged
love	hidden	attaining	Father	hearts
riches	wisdom			

Day 14: Being a Faithful Steward   Date: _____ /_____/_____

When you think of the words "good steward", most people assume that you are talking about a person who manages their finances well. However, this is only a fraction of the truth. It is important to be a good steward of everything God has assigned to us, not just our finances.

Paul is a great example of having good stewardship. A steward is a person who is a trusted and wise servant who manages or oversees a household. This household is not limited to a home. It can be any group or body of people or things. He was entrusted by God to preach the gospel to the Gentiles. He began to explain that the call to preach the gospel requires a person to be faithful. He declared that being a good steward was a gift. He then focuses on how he was in charge of explaining the mysteries of God. This is the work of the ministry and it's not limited to preachers, pastors and other clergy staff. Your home is a ministry. Your marriage is a ministry. Your job certainly is a ministry. And every single part of servitude is ministry.

When you serve, you serve according to your gifts, not according to positions and power. For example, if God has gifted you to sing, then why would you serve in the Children's Ministry? (if working with children isn't your gift) You are about to mess up those children's life! If you are gifted to teach, then why are you operating on the sound equipment? Now none of the speakers are working properly. I'm just using these as examples, but you should clearly see that operating outside the realm of your gifts and callings has the power to disrupt the things of God. In other words, you must be gifted or equipped so that your servitude can be effective in that area. If we were to be good stewards of the gifts and callings that God has given us, then we would save ourselves and others a headache. Additionally, you would advance the Kingdom of God in the earth.

If you don't know what your gifts and callings are, then ask God to reveal them to you. It's just that simple. He will show them to you in due time. All you have to do is trust that He will be faithful to show you the gifts that lay dormant within you. For those of you who know what your gifts are, are you using them for God's glory or are you withholding something that could bless Him and others?

I encourage you to be good stewards over what God has given you. Plant, water, and build by using your gifts. Ask God to anoint your gifts because it's time for activation. It's time out for sitting on the sidelines watching people honor God. You have the right and responsibility to honor God with what you have as well. Spend some time meditating in how you can please the Lord. Thank Him for what you have...material and spiritual. Ask the Lord to help you become a better steward.

Scripture References:

"Let a man so consider us as servants of Christ and stewards of the mysteries of God. Moreover, it is required in stewards that one be found faithful." (1 Corinthians 4:1-2, NKJV)

"But if anyone does not provide for his own, and especially for those of his household, he has denied the faith and is worse than an unbeliever." (1 Timothy 5:8, NKJV)

"As each one has received a gift, minister it to one another, as good stewards of the manifold grace of God." (1 Peter 4:10, NKJV)

Prayer:
Creator of my being, I praise and glorify your holy name. I seek your face today because I need your guidance. I need you to reveal the gifts you have given me so that I may use them for your glory. Open my eyes to see what you have graced me with. Teach me how to be a good steward over those things. Show me how to be responsible and dedicated. Take away any form of selfishness that you may find in me. Teach me to serve you and your people. I desire to be effective in the Kingdom of God. Use me for your will and for your glory. Show me the need that people may have. If there is anything within me that can fulfill the need of your people, reveal it to me so that I can surrender it back to you. I love you, worship you, and adore you. In Jesus' name, I pray, amen.

Personal Study/Application:
Write a list of gifts God has given to you. How could those gifts glorify God and edify His Kingdom?

_____

_____

_____

_____

_____

_____

_____

_____

_____

_____

_____

_____

_____

_____

_____

_____

_____

_____

_____

_____

Additionally, write down a list of things or people in which you are a steward. Examine your stewardship. Could there be improvements? If so, write them down here, then pray accordingly.

_____

_____

_____

Day 14: Being a Faithful Steward

Here are some words that pertains to being a faithful steward. The letters of the words below are jumbled. Figure out what the word is and write it on the blank line provided. Listed below are hints in the form of definitions or descriptions.

1 EUSLUF _____

2 TOTNIECMMM _____

3 TUFILAFH _____

4 NVSATER _____

5 DEADECDIT _____

6 EDELRA _____

7 ANCLGLI _____

8 PELRNSSOIBE _____

9 ENSLATT _____

10 IFSGT _____

11 EVIG _____

12 NAGEAM _____

1. able to be used for a practical purpose or in several ways

2. an engagement or obligation that restricts freedom of action

3. royal, constant, and steadfast

4. a person who performs duties for others

5. devoted to a task or purpose

6. the person who leads or commands a group, organization, or country.

7. a strong inner impulse toward a particular course of action

8. having an obligation to do something, or having control over or care for someone

9. a special often athletic, creative, or artistic aptitude

10. a natural ability or talent

11. provide or supply with.

12. be in charge of

Week 3:

Manifesting God's Glory

Day 15: The Fruit of the Spirit   Date: _____ /_____/_____

If you know me personally, then you would know that I love to study the Word of God and researching words with its original meaning in Hebrew (for the Old Testament) and Greek (for the New Testament). I do this because I gain more knowledge, understanding, and revelation of the Word when I study. The King James Version (KJV) of the Bible was the first "authorized" English Bible. When words are translated into another language, sometimes the meaning can be lost or easily misinterpreted. The words may be right, but the understanding may be unfruitful. Moreover, the meaning of a word in any language can change over time. For example, the word "meat" used to mean food in general. In the KJV, God gave Adam and Eve permission to eat from the fruit of the trees (except one). And He said that the fruit of those trees and the herbs from the ground is given to them for meat. Clearly, fruit from a tree and herbs from the ground are not animal flesh (Genesis 1:29, KJV) which is what the word "meat" means today. The word "nice" used to mean silly, foolish, or simple. Today, it's more of a compliment. So, when I study the Word with its original meaning, I find the real meaning of the context of scripture. If you would like to study in this manner, I suggest you get the Strong's Concordance. It's rich in revelation. Regarding today's focus on the Fruit of the Spirit, I'd like to share with you what I found when I looked up each word that pertains to the Fruit of the Spirit. This will give you a better understanding of how the Holy Spirit manifests Himself. Here are the main points of what I found for each word.

Love *(agape)*: "To love, to have affectionate regard, goodwill and benevolence." This simply takes away the feelings of "happiness". This kind of love has nothing to do with what or how we feel, but how we treat one another.

Joy *(chara)*: "Rejoicing or gladness." "The joy which the Holy Spirit imparts." Sounds fair enough. I looked at the synonyms which are "good, cheer, and gladness of heart." Then I looked at the antonyms, it said "distress, pain, and sorrow." I don't know about you, but I've been stressed in a few areas of my life. So now I know that stress is not a manifestation of the Holy Spirit, and I need to release stress immediately.

Peace *(Eirene)*: "wholeness, soundness, health, well-being, prosperity." Wait...prosperity too? So, prosperity has a deeper meaning than financial? Do you see where I'm going with this?

Longsuffering (patience) *(makrothumia)*: "forbearance or fortitude; Self-restraint before proceeding to action." "The quality of a person who is able to avenge himself yet refrains from doing so." So, I can feel a certain way and not act upon it and by doing that, I am showing mercy towards someone? Interesting!

Gentleness *(chrestotes)*: – "usefulness, benign (noncancerous or aggressive), excellence (in character or demeanor) goodness, kindness." Again, this has nothing to do with how we feel. But it involves how we act towards God or someone else. The closer we are to Him, the gentler we are in our actions towards others.

Goodness *(agathos)*: "Active goodness" This means that it must be ongoing or established; not just a thought or an intention but never doing it.

Faith *(pistis)*: "Firm persuasion, to win over, conviction in the truth." If this is the manifestation of the Holy Spirit, then we know that He is proving to us that we are growing in Him. Anything contrary to this is the opposite of faith. Without faith, how can we please God?

Meekness (praotes): "Gentleness by implying humility" Not just only are we expected to be good and kind, but this manifestation of the Spirit describes our character while being good and kind – humility!

Temperance (self-control) *(egkrateia)*: "Continence, Temperance." One of the synonyms is "sufficiency." The antonyms are "excess, self-indulgence, and senselessness." This one sounds like it is required for you to manage something with and regarding yourself.

Today's devotional being shared this way accomplishes two of my goals: 1) to teach you the meaning of the Fruit of the Spirit and 2) to show you how beneficial it is to STUDY the Word of God! Now that you have a clear meaning of what the fruit means, you can seek God on how to apply this to your life and ask God to manifest His fruit in you! Study, study, study! You never know what else you might learn even if you know a lot about a subject!

Scripture References:

"But the fruit of the Spirit is love, joy, peace, longsuffering, kindness, goodness, faithfulness, gentleness, self-control. Against such there is no law." (Galatians 5:22-23, NKJV)

"Be diligent to present yourself approved to God, a worker who does not need to be ashamed, rightly dividing the word of truth." (2 Timothy 2:15, NKJV)

Prayer:

Dear Lord, you are the head of my life and the author and finisher of my faith. Thank you for sending your Holy Spirit down from heaven and allowing the Holy Spirit to rest in me. Manifest your fruit within me. Create in me a clean heart and fill it with love, joy, peace, longsuffering, gentleness, goodness, faithfulness, meekness, and self-control. Also, fill me with your revelation and show me how to study your Word. Allow me to go deeper in your Word to have a full understanding of what you want to communicate to me. Help me to be careful to rightly divide the Word of God with clarity and understanding. In Jesus' name, amen.

Personal Study/Application:

Complete your own Bible study on the Fruit of the Spirit. Find a scripture that talks about each manifestation of the Spirit. How can you apply the scriptures to your life?

Love

_____

_____

_____

_____

_____

_____

Joy

_____

_____

_____

_____

_____

_____

Peace

_____

_____

_____

_____

_____

_____

Longsuffering (patience)

_____

_____

_____

_____

_____

_____

Gentleness

_____

_____

_____

_____

_____

_____

Goodness

_____

_____

_____

_____

_____

_____

Faith

_____

_____

_____

_____

_____

_____

Meekness

_____

_____

_____

_____

_____

_____

Temperance (self-control)

_____

_____

_____

_____

_____

_____

Quote

"Plants are more courageous than almost all human beings: an orange tree would rather die than produce lemons, whereas instead of dying the average person would rather be someone they are not."

— Mokokoma Mokhonoana

Day 15: The Fruit of the Spirit

Provide the word that best matches each clue.

1 _____ Self-restraint before proceeding to action

2 _____ Continence

3 _____ usefulness, excellence (in character or demeanor)

4 _____ Firm persuasion, to win over, conviction in the truth

5 _____ wholeness, soundness, health, well-being, prosperity

6 _____ Gentleness by implying humility

7 _____ Active goodness

8 _____ to have affectionate regard

9 _____ gladness

goodness	joy	peace
meekness	faith	love
gentleness	longsuffering (patience)	temperance (self-control)

Day 16: Obedience   Date: _____ /_____/_____

The Bible has a lot to say about obedience. All the way back to the story of Adam and Eve, obedience played an important role in their relationship with God. In fact, the concept of obedience was revealed before then. On day one, God said, "Let there be light." And light obeyed Him. Everything that God spoke into existence obeyed the voice of God. The earth was formed in obedience to God. The waters conformed to the shape of His calling. The grass grew to the capacity of His command. Everything obeys God. Everything above the earth, in the earth, and below the earth. If something that is non-living submits to God's authority, then don't you think that we should submit to God's will also? We are His greatest creation, you know. Yet we can be the most disobedient creatures who God as ever created.

The Hebrew word for obey is "shema" which means to hear or listen. It calls for a physical action or response. In the Greek, there are 2 words for obey. The first one is "hupotasso". It is a military term and it means "to rank under". The other Greek word is "hupakouo". This means "to listen to". So, we gather here that obedience is a position as well as an action or response. Better yet, we should position ourselves to respond according to God's direction and purpose.

Jesus is the greatest example of obedience. Even some of the greatest people in the Bible often had issues with obeying God. Jesus says, "If you love me, then you'll keep my commandments." (John 14:15) Obedience is an act of love and it's also an act of worship. Remember that salvation is a gift and we don't earn it through obeying. Obedience should come from the heart of the believer. Lastly, there are blessings that follows obedience. For it is better to obey than to sacrifice. I'm sure you have heard that before. Many Christians believe this means that it is better to obey God, then not to because something bad might happen. Did I get that right? Well, here is another revelation to go along with that. It was the law that required God's people to offer a sacrifice. The Lord is saying that it is better to obey God than to offer a sacrifice unto Him as if the ritual of sacrificing is more important than the heart of obedience. God is more concerned about your heart. Imagine if you were to sacrifice an animal in the name of repentance, but you know that you're going to commit that sin again. Do you really think that God cares about that sacrifice? Nope! If we were to be obedient first, then we wouldn't have to worry about a sacrifice. Commit in your fast TODAY that you want to live a lifestyle of obedience.

Scripture References:

"Now therefore, if you will indeed obey My voice and keep My covenant, then you shall be a special treasure to Me above all people; for all the earth is Mine." (Exodus 19:5, NKJV)

"Children, obey your parents in the Lord, for this is right. Honor your father and mother," which is the first commandment with promise: that it may be well with you and you may live long on the earth." (Ephesians 6:1-3, NKJV)

Prayer:

Dear God, I submit my heart to you. You have the authority to change my heart so that it can line up with your will. I position myself with humility so that I may obey your Word. I step out on faith and encourage myself to trust you. When you speak to me, allow me to listen. Give me the boldness to trust you and complete any assignment that you have for me. Lord my worship is for real. Forgive me for times in which I was not obedient to you or anyone you have set over me. Empower me to live a life in accordance with your Word and obedient to your commands. In Jesus' name, amen.

Personal Study/Application:

Take a moment to examine all the areas of your life. Are there any areas in your life in where you find yourself in disobedience? If so, why do you think disobedience is present in that area? Besides repenting, what else can you do to change this?

_____

_____

_____

_____

_____

_____

_____

_____

_____

Day 16: Obedience

Answer the questions to the devotional you just read by providing the letter of the word which best answers the question.

1 ___ Obedience is an act of what?
   A. LOVE   B. MANKIND   C. HUMILITY   D. TO HEAR OR LISTEN

2 ___ What is better than sacrifice?
   A. MANKIND   B. HUMILITY   C. TO LISTEN TO   D. OBEY

3 ___ How should Christians position themselves?
   A. MANKIND   B. JESUS   C. HUMILITY   D. LOVE

4 ___ What does the Greek word "hupotasso" mean?
   A. TO RANK UNDER   B. TO HEAR OR LISTEN   C. HUMILITY   D. LOVE

5 ___ Who is the greatest example of obedience
   A. OBEY   B. LOVE   C. HUMILITY   D. JESUS

6 ___ Who or what obeyed God first?
   A. TO RANK UNDER   B. ANIMALS   C. HUMILITY   D. OBEDIENCE

7 ___ What does the Hebrew word "shema" means?
   A. LOVE   B. ANIMALS   C. TO HEAR OR LISTEN   D. OBEDIENCE

8 ___ Worship is a form of what?
   A. MANKIND   B. HUMILITY   C. OBEDIENCE   D. JESUS

9 ___ Which creation has a tendency to disobey God?
   A. OBEDIENCE   B. HUMILITY   C. MANKIND   D. OBEY

10 ___ What does the Greek word "hupakouo" mean?
   A. MANKIND   B. TO LISTEN TO   C. ANIMALS   D. OBEDIENCE

Day 17: Communication

Date: _____ /_____/_____

God is a great communicator, and it has been His mission to commune with His creation before the fall of man. However, man has not been great at communicating as he or she should, and it has affected our relationships with the Lord and others. Even Christians have problems communicating with each other. Husbands and wives often struggle to understand each other. When prayer is not the most popular choice within the church, man has trouble communicating with God.

The Bible says that life and death are in the power of the tongue (Proverbs 18:21). We must be careful with what we speak because it has the power to make or break something or someone. The Bible also says that we must be swift to hear, slow to speak, and slow to wrath (James 1:19). This is the other element that is involved with communication – listening. So, we have the power of words and the ability to hear. Both of which are important to effectively communicate. We must make sure that we are using each skill appropriately because what we say and how we listen to others is important to God.

The problem comes in when we have these things out of order. We don't have control over our methods of communication. We are to be quick to hear and slow to speak. Instead, we are slow to listen and quick to speak our mind. And what is the result? Confusion. Hurt or angry feelings, and people who believe that they are misunderstood.

You cannot assume that you already know what another person wants or needs without them telling you or before you ask. People also make the terrible mistake of thinking that what they have to say should be what others want to hear. So, we have something to offer, but we don't have the capacity to receive (hear). That can be very dangerous. To hear or understand someone, you must listen and listening takes effort.

I remember teaching my children how to talk, read, and write. At some point, I had to teach them how to listen. I understood that they heard me, but it was evident that they did not listen. The funny thing is that I must reiterate this teaching at every stage of their youth. I remember telling my son to take out the trash. I knew he heard me because he acknowledged it by saying, "Yes sir." But hours later, the trash still hadn't been taken out. I said, "Son, did you hear what I said about the trash?" He said, "Yes sir, you told me not to forget to take the trash out. I haven't forgotten daddy." I said, "No son; I told you to take the trash out." I learned a 2-fold lesson that day. Although my son heard me say something about the trash, if he would have listened to the words I used, and the tone of my voice, then he would have known that I meant for him to take the trash out right now. Lesson # 1, you must listen. Then I second guessed myself for a moment. I thought to myself, "Did I tell him not to forget to take the trash out, or did I tell him to take the trash out right now?" And then it hit me. Lesson # 2, you must communicate clearly. If I told him not to forget, then he could have perceived that to mean, "you don't have to do it right now." It's important to say what you mean and mean what you say. Being slow to speak is also wise. God wants us to choose our words carefully. He wants us to be mature in our speech so that it can reflect

His relationship with us. We must strip ourselves from corrupt communication, profanity, negative and offensive comments. In return, we are to speak blessings and things that are praise-worthy.

Scripture References:
"He who answers a matter before he hears *it*, it *is* folly and shame to him." (Proverbs 18:13, NKJV)

"Let the words of my mouth and the meditation of my heart be acceptable in Your sight, O LORD, my strength and my Redeemer." (Psalm 19:14, NKJV)

"*Let* your speech always *be* with grace, seasoned with salt, that you may know how you ought to answer each one." (Colossians 4:6, NKJV)

"A soft answer turns away wrath, but a harsh word stirs up anger. The tongue of the wise uses knowledge rightly, but the mouth of fools pours forth foolishness." (Proverbs 15:1-2, NKJV)

Prayer:
Dear God, when I am communicating with others, allow me to hear divinely and correctly. When I hear, cause me to understand. Give me wisdom to clarify anything within any conversation in which I may have doubt. Remove all confusion so communication can take place. Most of all Lord, help me with my communication with you. When you speak, allow me to hear your voice. Quite the voice of the enemy and amplify your voice in

my ear. Lord, I want to hear from you often. Speak to me Lord. I pray in Jesus' name, amen.

Personal Study/Application:

Pay attention to your words and your hearing today. Take the time to journal how you have refrained from speaking negatively. If you would have said something, how different would that conversation might have gone. Listen closely today. Try to understand what is being said or asked of you. Is there anything about your speech or hearing that you may need to work on? Write down your findings and pray over your concerns.

_____

_____

_____

_____

_____

_____

_____

_____

_____

_____

_____

_____

Day 17: Communication

Listed below are some tips for effective communication. Read the prompt and decide if it is concerning listening or hearing.

1 ___ Don't rush or cut the other person off.
A. LISTENING   B. SPOKEN

2 ___ Try to block out distractions.
A. SPOKEN   B. LISTENING

3 ___ Ask questions to show you are interested and to clarify things you aren't sure of.
A. LISTENING   B. SPOKEN

4 ___ Don't talk just to fill the silence.
A. SPOKEN   B. LISTENING

5 ___ Don't focus on rehearsing what you will say next.
A. SPOKEN   B. LISTENING

6 ___ If the person expresses strong feelings, try to acknowledge them without becoming offended or angry yourself.
A. LISTENING   B. SPOKEN

7 ___ Be respectful.
A. SPOKEN   B. LISTENING

8 ___ Be forgiving.
A. SPOKEN   B. LISTENING

9 ___ Speak clearly, avoiding jargon and confusing ramblings.
A. LISTENING   B. SPOKEN

10 ___ Smile and look the other person in the eye naturally
A. SPOKEN   B. LISTENING

11 ___ Look for common ground.
A. LISTENING   B. SPOKEN

12 ___ Express appreciation and encouragement
A. LISTENING   B. SPOKEN

13 ___ Apologize when needed
A. SPOKEN   B. LISTENING

14 ___ Use "I" statements instead of accusing.
A. LISTENING   B. SPOKEN

Day 18: Believers Prayer

Date: _____ /_____/_____

Today, we are going to keep it simple. Everybody needs prayer, particularly believers. I know that the enemy's job is to kill, steal, and destroy, and it seems like the enemy is doing his job very well. Which makes me ask, are we doing ours? It seems like so many of our brothers and sisters are falling by the ways of the world. What is really going on here? Are we not strong enough to surpass the enemy's devices? Do we no longer have the desire to serve the living God? Obviously, it could be either one or both. So, we should keep our brothers and sisters in prayer.

In addition to those that seem to have given up, we have our other brothers and sisters who are trying to hold on to God for dear life! You never know what people are going through behind closed doors. Some people will tell you their problems, but they won't tell you all of it. That "all of it" part, is what has them secretly trapped. So, let's pray and believe God for our brothers and sisters. Let's pray for one another. Make this day a selfless day and fast on somebody else' behalf. Remember, this is a secret that's kept between you and God.

NOTE: I know that we are focusing on praying for believers of the Faith. However, don't be afraid to include future believers – the people we are believing God will bring into salvation. They need your prayers as well. Today, pray for all family members, friends, co-workers, neighbors, etc. Don't leave anybody out. Bless somebody today. Allow the Holy Spirit to lead you on who to bless and how you can be a blessing to them.

Scripture References:

"Therefore, if anyone *is* in Christ, *he is* a new creation; old things have passed away; behold, all things have become new." (2 Corinthians 5:17, NKJV)

"If we confess our sins, He is faithful and just to forgive us *our* sins and to cleanse us from all unrighteousness." (1 John 1:9, NKJV)

"And you will be hated by all for My name's sake. But he who endures to the end will be saved." (Matthew 10:22, NKJV)

Prayer:

Father, you know all things. You know what's going on with your people. I pray that your people do not fall for the enemy's tricks. You are a keeper. Let them acknowledge that you are a keeper. Let them count it all joy when they fall into many temptations. Let them have a hunger and thirst for righteousness. Give them a mind to seek your face. Soften their heart so that they can fall in love with you. Open their eyes so that they can see where they are and where they need to be. Restore the believers' hope in you. Give them hinds feet to press forward and continue to run their race. Remind them that they will reap in due season if they do not give up. Renew them like an eagle and help them soar again above whatever that has weighed them down. Help them get back in the race and stay on the journey until the end. Save our families oh God, cause them to run to you for repentance. Deliver them from all their troubles. Mend broken marriages back together again. Clear their communication and allow them to forgive one another, cover one another, and restore their union. I lift up the children oh God as they are faced with many negative influences. Send your angels to watch over them and protect them. Lead them to a path in which they can follow. Give them a heart to want to serve you God. I cover their minds against the spirit of suicide. They are worthy and valuable. They have a place to fit in because they can fit into your arms. I come against the spirit of bullying. They have a friend in you Lord. I lift the drug addicts to you God. Some of them you have called and some you have chosen. Allow them to hear your call. Give them the courage to rebel against the tie and loose them to freedom! In Jesus' name, amen.

Personal Study/Application:

Make a prayer list of all the people who God has put on your heart to pray for. Call them out by name and make your request known to God. Don't be afraid to go into warfare. The people need your prayers. Make this prayer about others. Do not mention anything about yourself. Remember that this prayer is a secret between you and God.

_____

_____

_____

_____

_____

_____

_____

_____

_____

Day 18: Believers Prayer

Here is a list of people who you can pray for. Pray for them as you mark them off.

```
Z G S K C A T T A T S I R O R R E T C M
S R E D N O P S E R T S R I F T S P Z F
L W R Q G B D F G W D A D N S D C N V W
P S T U C O T U O F R L U N U K U E C F
R T K G C B E Z V S U P R E A C H E R S
H V Y T E C A E E W G N D W I V E S P R
X C O W G L C I R B A E M F M N L S M G
Z R K N M J H C N O D R U Q A M Y R P E
S Q C H P Y E J M F D D S W B F Z E F K
J U W N H E R W E J I L R F R Q D R K U
M C D M A W S T N L C I M E L O K E Y N
N A M E R I F E T A T H F T P K X D F O
G Y T T M X C V Q W S C P H M K K R Q O
O S P S A O I F T Y G X I S E G D U J K
S Y Z A C Q Q H H E M L C D W T J M F J
T B D X I R A Z I R E Z P N D R I W J N
O R V J S Z P I H S R E D A E L D V Z Z
L F D X T N K S Z G N H U S B A N D S F
I H B V S P X L Q T E E N A G E R S A K
P D M T N E M E C R O F N E W A L P Y Q
```

CHILDREN	JUDGES	PILOTS
DOCTORS	LAW ENFORCEMENT	PREACHERS
DRUG ADDICTS	LAWYERS	TEACHERS
FIREMAN	LEADERSHIP	TEENAGERS
FIRST RESPONDERS	MURDERERS	TERRORIST ATTACKS
GOVERNMENT	PEDOPHILES	WIVES
HUSBANDS	PHARMACISTS	

The Daniel Way: 21 Days of Fasting and Prayer to Reboot Your Entire Being

Day 19: Relationships   Date: _____ /_____/_____

God has always been about relationships. He created the whole world for relationships. He created man to have a relationship with Him. He commanded Adam to have a relationship with the earth. Then He created woman to have a relationship with Adam. God has always been concerned about how people treat others. Jesus regularly explained His relationship with the Father. The Word explains the relationship in marriage and the relationship of parents and children. The Word also explains the relationship between supervisors and employees. It just goes on-and-on. It is safe to say that the entire Bible is about relationships.

When it comes to our relationship with God, Jesus teaches us that we should always put God first and that we should love Him with our entire being. I find it funny that so many people are going through so much in their lives that they don't have to. All they have to do is surrender to the Lord. They would grow to love Him and build a close relationship. Surrendering to God doesn't mean that problems will go away, but with Christ living inside of you, He will teach you ways to handle them. You can't expect for people to change if they are not willing to surrender to God. Instead, they continue to build their relationships with fantasies and end up being deceived.

The only way you can love your neighbor the way God intended is to have a relationship with God yourself. God first, then others. This includes marriage as well. How can a husband build a relationship with his wife if he doesn't understand God's relationship with His people? Today, let's focus on relationships, either building them or repairing them in the love of Christ.

Scripture References:

"And you shall love the Lord your God with all your heart and with all your soul and with all your mind and with all your strength Mark 12:30

"For all the law is fulfilled in one word, *even* in this: "You shall love your neighbor as yourself." Galatians 5:14

Prayer:

Father, thank you for pursuing a relationship with me. In times of disobedience you never gave up on me and you never stopped loving me. You are love and you continue to show your love. Thank you for investing so much to have a relationship with me. Because your love is living in me, I can show the same love to you and others. Father, I pray for marriages. Help them to communicate effectively and relate to one another. I come against the spirit of divorce, miscommunication, misunderstanding, discord, and separation. Let no man nor devil cause disunity. I pray for the relationships between parents and their children. Father teach the parents how to teach their children your ways. Allow the parents to open their hearts and listen to and understand their children. Allow the children to become wiser and listen to their parents. Let them know that obedience is required, and that God blesses them according to their obedience. Mend broken relationships between parents/guardians and their children. I pray for relationships between co-workers. I bind the spirit of jealousy and loose the spirit of unity and love in the workplace. I pray for relationships between supervisors and their staff. Let every task be completed for the glory of God. I pray that believers will respect their supervisors and that supervisors will not be partial towards their staff. Lord, I pray for relationships between clergy and church members. I pray they can find a common goal to reach within their missions and stay centered around you. Lastly, help your people understand how to build godly relationships with others. Thank you for the relationships that I have and for the people you have sent my way to help me grow in this journey. I pray that you will continue to bless them. In Jesus' name, amen.

Personal Study/Application:

Write down some relationships that you would like to work on. What about those relationships concern you? Write everything down and pray concerning those relationships.

_____

_____

_____

_____

_____

_____

_____

_____

_____

_____

_____

Day 19: Relationships

Below the blank puzzle grid is a list of positive words that promotes healthy relationships. Place the words in the correct place on the grid. Tip: Start with letter sizes that have the fewest words. So if there are only 2 words with 7 letters and 5 words with 4 letters, try placing the 7 letter words first.

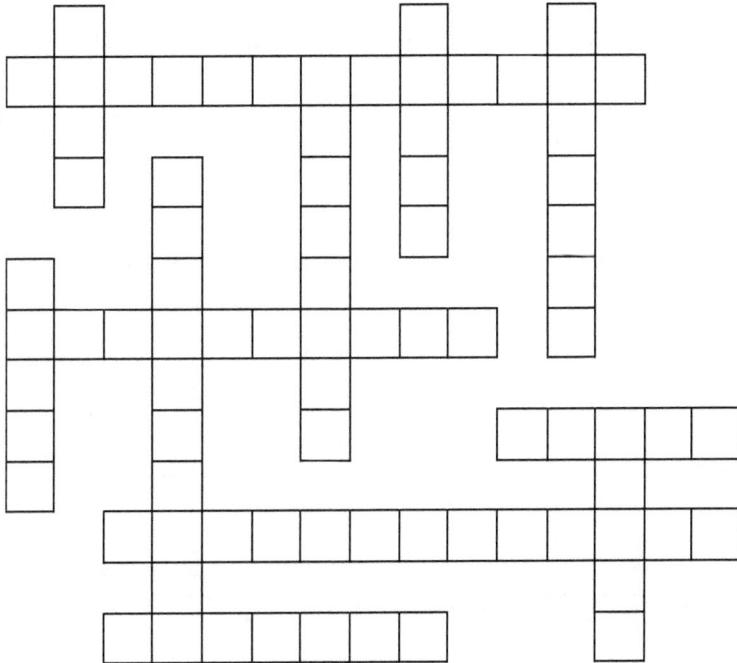

4 Letters	TRUST	8 Letters	13 Letters
LOVE		INTIMACY	UNDERSTANDING
	7 Letters		COMMUNICATION
5 Letters	RESPECT	10 Letters	
HONOR	LOYALTY	OBSERVANCE	
VALUE		ACCEPTANCE	
UNITY			

The Daniel Way: 21 Days of Fasting and Prayer to Reboot Your Entire Being

Day 20: Expectation   Date: _____ /_____/_____

We must first believe, have faith that God is...and God can. Expect God to do great things in your life as you continue to fast and pray. God has NOT overlooked you! You are special to Him and He is concerned about what you are concerned about. Don't ever doubt this fact for a second! Don't allow the enemy to steal your joy or your expectation. Faith is required!

Scripture Reference:

"For the earnest expectation of the creation eagerly waits for the revealing of the sons of God." (Romans 8:19, NKJV)

"but a certain fearful expectation of judgment, and fiery indignation which will devour the adversaries." (Hebrews 10:27, NKJV)

"Therefore, you also be ready, for the Son of Man is coming at an hour you do not expect." (Luke 12:40, NKJV)

Prayer:

Lord, I praise you and lift up your holy name. As I lift you up, pour out unto me that I may not lose faith in you. Stretch out my expectation and establish my faith. Because I am confident in your Word, I will not lose hope. I expect your will to be done in my life and in my family's life. Father, I am expecting you to perform miracles. I expect my loved ones to surrender their ways to your ways. I expect blessing to pour out from the windows of heaven. I expect blessing in which I do not have room to receive. Thank you oh God for increasing my faith. Doubt, I curse you at the root. You shall no longer hinder my prayers and my faith. Move out of my way; I am here to overcome you. I believe that God will be faithful to His Word. God is not a man that He should lie. So, I trust and depend solely on God! I live in a state of expectation and keep my faith and hope alive in my heart. I believe what God has said and I will continue to do so until I see the manifestation of His promises! In Jesus' name, amen.

Personal Study/Application:
Make a list of your expectations from God. Examine the list carefully and pray about each one. Don't forget to carry your faith while you seek the Lord.

_____

_____

_____

_____

_____

_____

_____

_____

_____

_____

_____

_____

_____

_____

Day 20: Expectation

Find the hidden words that are associated with expectation.

```
F  D  Y  V  E  N  G  X  P  X  K  I  C  B  I  U  K  J  V  M
A  U  G  A  D  P  W  D  E  L  I  V  E  R  A  N  C  E  J  K
P  B  G  Y  U  R  O  J  E  R  I  K  E  F  I  O  D  O  H  P
A  E  U  K  Q  L  F  Y  N  S  K  C  Z  B  Y  L  A  E  H  O
R  C  L  N  W  C  Q  Y  V  G  W  Z  X  K  A  Z  K  S  F  E
M  Y  Q  R  D  A  W  Z  V  Z  T  D  T  V  R  D  E  V  Y  B
R  H  S  W  C  A  I  T  F  P  X  F  S  A  P  Y  T  B  M  G
Y  C  R  E  M  M  N  T  U  S  R  J  F  M  M  I  F  O  G  M
J  N  S  E  L  Z  D  C  A  A  W  O  T  R  H  T  I  A  F  O
C  K  A  H  A  C  K  Z  E  V  G  A  V  U  M  N  R  Y  E  D
U  P  L  M  O  I  A  M  C  H  W  S  G  I  W  K  A  V  S  X
S  B  V  Q  N  U  I  R  G  Q  G  K  Y  Y  S  L  E  B  J  J
I  M  A  Z  V  A  W  G  I  N  W  I  L  N  H  I  K  P  H  M
G  E  T  K  L  Q  K  G  I  M  Y  N  S  W  L  Z  O  W  S  O
M  W  I  C  R  A  N  S  Z  S  Y  K  H  E  A  O  U  N  W  V
O  H  O  N  J  D  S  E  Z  J  U  N  B  V  R  C  L  V  T  E
C  R  N  W  M  E  E  D  E  R  Z  N  K  E  V  I  E  C  E  R
P  M  T  M  L  U  K  X  I  W  W  K  B  P  J  J  F  E  N  W
R  S  C  B  C  D  F  V  W  H  D  Q  E  E  O  G  M  C  N  B
R  E  T  L  E  H  S  O  S  H  Q  N  X  D  U  B  S  B  P  O
```

ABUNDANCE	EAGER	MOVE	REDEEM
ASK	FAITH	PRAY	SALVATION
BELIEVE	HEAL	PROCLAIM	SHELTER
BLESSINGS	MERCY	PROVISION	WAIT
DELIVERANCE	MIRACLES	RECEIVE	YES

The Daniel Way: 21 Days of Fasting and Prayer to Reboot Your Entire Being

Day 21: Release

Today is the last day of the fast. It's time to release. Before you make your divine exit, I want to share a quick story with you. Do you remember Rhoda in the Bible? She's only mentioned one time in the Bible. In Acts 12:12-15, it talks about how she and other guests were praying in her home. When Peter was miraculously freed from prison, he went straight to her home, where the saints were interceding for Peter. What Rhoda was praying for was knocking at her door! Did you get that revelation? She was the only one who was released from the burden of praying for Peter as everyone else was still praying. Even when their prayer was answered and was staring them in the face, some still didn't believe because they said that it was not Peter, but only his spirit. They didn't understand the power of release.

We must be in tune with God to know when we are released from something. In fact, you can be released before you see it come to pass. How do you do that? You see it in faith. Jesus was released from His burden on the cross. Enoch was released when God took him. Moses was released before seeing the promise land. You can be released from a burden or released from praying about something. Take time to seek God and determine if you can be released from the fast. If you need to stay in a fasted state, do so! Whenever you are released, don't throw away this book! Keep it near and as the Lord direct you to fast in the future, refer to the Bible and this book as a companion. Remember fasting is a part of your Christian lifestyle. It's not a one-time thing.

On this 21st day of your fast, look over the past 20 days and determine a need you have that was not covered and fast for that need as today's topic. Write your own devotional; find scripture references that support your topic; and write your prayer.

Enjoy the Journey!

Devotional:

_____

_____

_____

_____

_____

_____

_____

_____

_____

_____

_____

_____

_____

_____

_____

_____

_____

_____

Scripture References:

_____

_____

_____

_____

_____

_____

_____

_____

_____

_____

_____

_____

_____

_____

_____

_____

_____

_____

_____

_____

_____

_____

_____

_____

_____

_____

Prayer:

_____

_____

_____

_____

_____

_____

_____

_____

_____

_____

_____

_____

_____

_____

_____

_____

_____

_____

_____

_____

_____

_____

Personal Study/Application:

Continue to meditate concerning your topic. Position yourself to hear from God. Write down anything the Holy Spirit reveals to you. Don't forget to thank Him for giving you the opportunity to make your request known unto Him.

_____

_____

_____

_____

_____

_____

_____

_____

_____

_____

_____

_____

_____

_____

_____

_____

_____

_____

_____
_____
_____
_____
_____
_____
_____
_____
_____
_____
_____
_____
_____
_____
_____
_____
_____
_____
_____
_____
_____
_____
_____
_____

Day 21: Release

Find the hidden words that are associated with release.

```
P  H  I  Q  B  L  P  J  F  S  C  A  K  R  X  X  E  G  I  G
O  Y  R  H  V  E  K  Z  K  U  O  D  F  N  W  U  N  Z  S  U
B  C  E  A  G  X  X  Q  A  T  U  C  Z  D  C  O  W  I  G  B
M  N  C  C  J  O  H  P  M  E  H  M  Y  S  I  Q  A  Q  Q  A
G  E  N  A  E  N  G  B  R  X  G  W  E  T  W  Z  L  L  Y  P
N  M  A  Y  N  E  S  L  W  C  O  R  U  M  Q  C  K  E  T  P
J  E  T  G  N  R  O  C  E  Q  H  L  A  A  Z  M  O  U  I  D
X  L  T  T  C  A  Q  N  J  M  O  F  Q  H  C  Y  U  R  N  E
B  C  I  N  T  T  R  T  O  S  A  M  U  N  C  B  T  N  U  L
Q  Y  U  A  Q  I  R  A  B  I  K  N  J  H  U  S  J  E  M  I
P  N  Q  M  T  O  V  A  N  L  T  S  C  T  L  A  I  F  M  V
H  Z  C  Z  F  N  X  I  I  S  T  A  T  I  M  V  P  D  I  E
M  V  A  T  Z  M  V  B  V  W  O  C  G  N  P  L  F  Z  X  R
W  O  T  T  C  N  E  N  B  A  X  M  E  R  U  A  A  C  W  A
G  R  D  Z  V  R  T  O  I  R  Q  S  M  E  U  O  T  L  Q  N
B  Q  X  E  A  Y  Q  D  I  G  T  G  K  D  G  P  M  I  U  C
V  R  L  T  E  S  X  R  V  Y  F  E  I  L  E  R  M  U  O  E
Q  D  I  I  G  R  E  A  W  B  I  C  O  I  K  R  E  O  I  N
M  O  L  K  A  D  F  P  E  X  E  M  P  T  I  O  N  Z  C  D
N  R  W  P  V  B  N  S  S  P  R  I  N  G  I  Y  N  Z  Y  O
```

ABSOLUTION	DISCHARGE	PARDON
ACQUITTANCE	EMANCIPATION	RANSOM
AMNESTY	EXEMPTION	RELIEF
BAIL	EXONERATION	RESCUE
CLEMENCY	FREEDOM	SPRING
COMPURGATION	IMMUNITY	WALKOUT

The Daniel Way: 21 Days of Fasting and Prayer to Reboot Your Entire Being

Answer Key

Days 1 - 21

Day 1: Repentance

Find the hidden words that are associated with repentance.

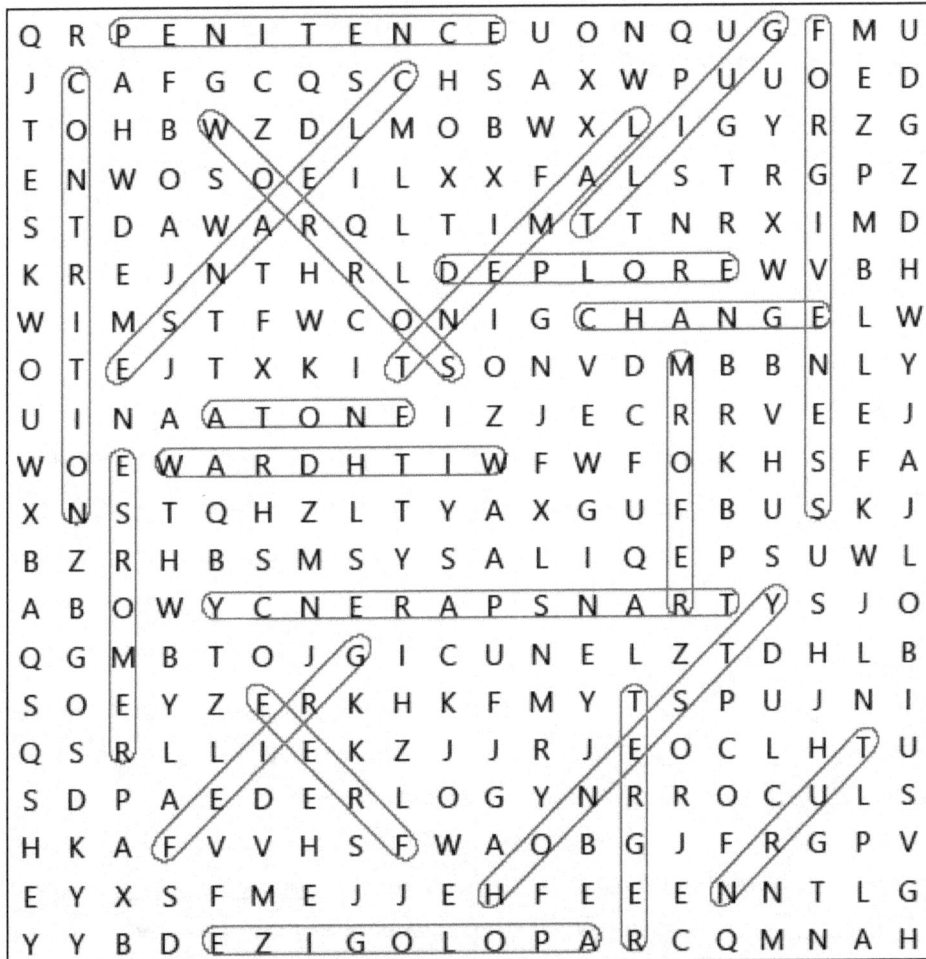

```
Q R P E N I T E N C E U O N Q U G F M U
J C A F G C Q S C H S A X W P U U O E D
T O H B W Z D L M O B W X L I G Y R Z G
E N W O S O E I L X X F A L S T R G P Z
S T D A W A R Q L T I M T T N R X I M D
K R E J N T H R L D E P L O R E W V B H
W I M S T F W C O N I G C H A N G E L W
O T E J T X K I T S O N V D M B B N L Y
U I N A A T O N E I Z J E C R R V E E J
W O E W A R D H T I W F W F O K H S F A
X N S T Q H Z L T Y A X G U F B U S K J
B Z R H B S M S Y S A L I Q E P S U W L
A B O W Y C N E R A P S N A R T Y S J O
Q G M B T O J G I C U N E L Z T D H L B
S O E Y Z E R K H K F M Y T S P U J N I
Q S R L L I E K Z J J R J E O C L H T U
S D P A E D E R L O G Y N R R O C U L S
H K A F V V H S F W A O B G J F R G P V
E Y X S F M E J J E H F E E E N N T L G
Y Y B D E Z I G O L O P A R C Q M N A H
```

APOLOGIZE	DEPLORE	HONESTY	REMORSE
ATONE	FORGIVENESS	LAMENT	SORROW
CHANGE	FREE	PENITENCE	TRANSPARENCY
CLEANSE	GRIEF	REFORM	TURN
CONTRITION	GUILT	REGRET	WITHDRAW

Day 2: Purification

A number of words have been removed from the scripture and placed in a word bank. Use the words from the word bank to fill in the blanks in the scripture. Write the words in the blanks provided. Challenge yourself and try to complete this without using the hint.

"Therefore, since we have these (1) promises , dear friends, let us (2) purify ourselves from everything that (3) contaminates body and (4) spirit , perfecting holiness out of (5) reverence for God."
(**Hint:** 2 Corinthians 7:1, NIV)

"He went on: "What comes out of a person is what (6) defiles them. For it is from within, out of a person's heart, that evil thoughts come-sexual immorality, theft, murder, adultery, (7) greed , malice, deceit, lewdness, envy, slander, arrogance and folly. All these evils come from (8) inside and defile a person." (**Hint:** Mark 7:20 - 23, NIV)

" For the grace of God has appeared that offers salvation to all people. 12 It teaches us to say "(9) No " to ungodliness and worldly (10) passions , and to live (11) self-controlled, upright and godly lives in this present age, 13 while we wait for the blessed hope-the appearing of the glory of our great God and Savior, Jesus Christ, 14 who gave himself for us to (12) redeem us from all (13) wickedness and to purify for himself a people that are his very own, eager to do what is (14) good ." (**Hint:** Titus 2:11 - 14, NIV)

reverence	inside	contaminates	greed
redeem	promises	purify	good
No	defiles	spirit	self-controlled
passions	wickedness		

Day 3: Sanctification

Use the New King James Version (NKJV) to complete the crossword puzzle. Look up the scriptures that are listed under the Across and Down sections. Find the "important" word that coincides with today's fasting topic. Then write that word in the crossword puzzle.

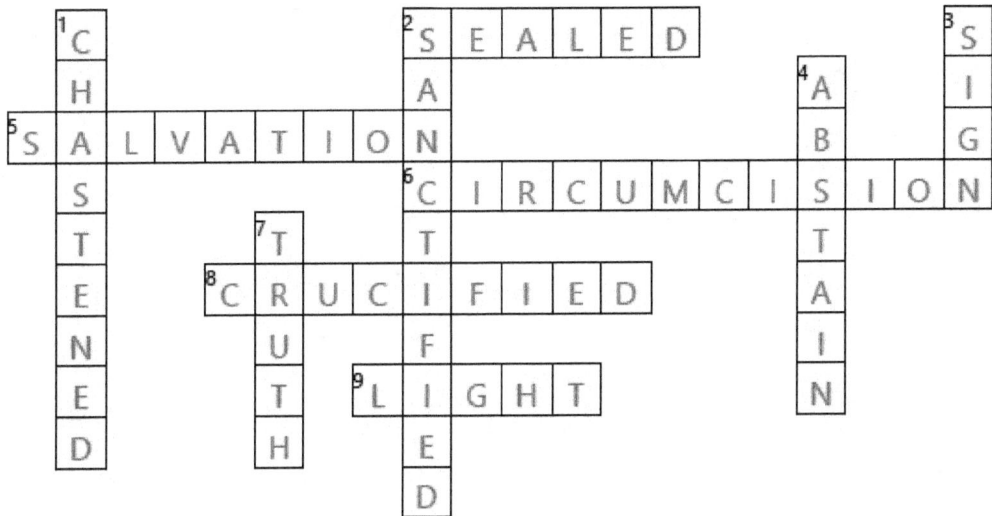

Crossword answers:

- 1 Down: CHASTENED
- 2 Across: SEALED / 2 Down: SAN...
- 3 Down: SIGN
- 4 Down: ABSTAIN
- 5 Across: SALVATION
- 6 Across: CIRCUMCISION / 6 Down: CIRCUMCISED
- 7 Down: TRUTH
- 8 Across: CRUCIFIED
- 9 Across: LIGHT

ACROSS

2. Ephesians 1:13
5. 1 Thessalonians 5:23
6. Colossians 2:11
8. Galatians 2:20
9. Acts 26:18

DOWN

2. Ephesians 1:13
5. 1 Thessalonians 5:23
6. Colossians 2:11
8. Galatians 2:20
9. Acts 26:18

Day 4: Adoration & Thanksgiving

The letters of the words below are jumbled. Figure out what the word is and write it on the blank line provided. Listed below are hints in forms of scriptures or definitions. All scriptures are from the New King James Version (NKJV).

1 MACYRRGE GRAMERCY

2 TBNINIEDECO BENEDICTION

3 ITOTYNMES TESTIMONY

4 ORITEINOGCN RECOGNITION

5 DETBSIENSEDN INDEBTEDNESS

6 HTAKSN THANKS

7 TETIBUR TRIBUTE

8 LGIBONATOI OBLIGATION

9 RIECOPAAIPTN APPRECIATION

10 IINVATOCNO INVOCATION

11 ITOIETNP PETITION

12 ISAREP PRAISE

13 ELGEARFNUSST GRATEFULNESS

14 RCDITE CREDIT

15 EAGCR GRACE

16 TEULNKSSAHNF THANKFULNESS

17 DIAGETRTU GRATITUDE

18 ANKIHTNSVGGI THANKSGIVING

19 NTEENLMWDACKOG ACKNOWLEDGMENT

20 BISLEGSN BLESSING

1. used to express gratitude or surprise
2. something that promotes goodness or well-being
3. Revelation 12:11
4. special notice or attention
5. something that is owed
6. 1 Thessalonians 5:18
7. 1 Chronicles 18:6
8. 2 Corinthians 9:5
9. a feeling or expression of admiration, approval, or gratitude
10. a calling upon for authority or justification
11. 1 Samuel 1:17
12. Exodus 15:2
13. appreciative of benefits received
14. 1 Peter 2:20
15. Genesis 6:8
16. Acts 24:3
17. the state of being grateful
18. Psalm 100:4
19. 1 Corinthians 16:18
20. Proverbs 10:22

Day 5: My Identity in Christ

The scripture below has been written in code. Use the hints in the decoder at the top of the page to help IDENTIFY the code (the letters on top are the correct answers, the letters on the bottom are the code, one has been solved for you). Then fill-in the correct letter in the blank space above each code letter in the text. Will you be able to find your "Identity in Christ?"

D	I	P	X	L	V	T	E	Q	U	K	W	Z	G	S	M	O	A	F	B	H	C	R	Y	N	J
A	B	C	D	E	F	G	H	I	J	K	L	M	N	O	P	Q	R	S	T	U	V	W	X	Y	Z

I have been crucified with Christ
"B URFH THHY VWJVBSBHA LBGU VUWBOG;

it is no longer I who live but
BG BO YQ EQYNHW B LUQ EBFH, TJG

Christ lives in me and the life
VUWBOG EBFHO BY PH; RYA GUH EBSH

which I now live in the flesh I live
LUBVU B YQL EBFH BY GUH SEHOU B EBFH

by faith in the Son of God who
TX SRBGU BY GUH OQY QS NQA, LUQ

loved me and gave Himself for me
EQFHA PH RYA NRFH UBPOHS SQW PH."

Galatians   NKJV
(NRERGBRYO 2:20, YKZF)

Day 6: Purpose for My Life

Find the hidden words that are associated with gifts and talents.

```
T  U  I  A  H  N  G  F  G  R  R  R  B  Z  P  R  A  Y  E  R
Y  D  G  K  N  Z  A  N  A  N  K  O  H  B  D  M  U  S  I  C
Y  B  J  N  M  D  R  Y  I  I  I  T  E  H  L  V  Y  H  D  I
B  W  M  L  I  C  Z  P  T  L  T  T  V  C  K  G  S  C  O  Q
Z  L  G  N  I  T  N  I  A  P  E  H  A  J  I  P  V  H  Q  U
K  Z  T  X  U  N  I  C  E  C  K  S  R  R  Z  V  N  B  W  Z
C  O  M  P  U  T  E  R  S  D  J  I  N  O  O  C  R  W  Z  E
V  F  Q  M  J  P  R  H  W  B  K  B  C  U  L  C  I  E  C  N
S  L  L  I  K  S  L  A  C  I  D  E  M  V  O  G  E  S  S  T
G  E  I  L  P  D  X  P  K  M  M  Z  C  P  S  C  N  D  E  R
A  X  S  D  B  T  E  A  C  H  I  N  G  H  T  O  K  C  L  E
Q  O  C  A  R  E  G  I  V  E  R  M  Z  O  K  Q  A  N  E  P
B  V  V  S  Q  K  Q  N  O  T  F  F  U  T  B  I  J  O  C  R
S  P  E  C  I  A  L  N  E  E  D  S  W  O  R  K  E  R  T  E
K  L  K  R  E  Z  R  T  F  U  A  Q  X  G  E  T  L  Z  R  N
X  H  W  V  K  M  B  Q  M  Z  J  F  I  R  O  F  D  L  I  E
N  O  I  T  A  R  T  S  I  N  I  M  D  A  Z  E  Q  V  C  U
W  V  G  A  R  D  E  N  I  N  G  E  Z  P  K  P  P  W  I  R
Q  Y  T  I  L  A  T  I  P  S  O  H  O  H  L  T  V  E  A  B
M  T  A  Z  C  O  O  K  I  N  G  I  B  Y  S  Z  I  O  N  X
```

ADMINISTRATION	DECORATING	HOSPITALITY	PRAYER
CAREGIVER	ELECTRICIAN	MEDICAL SKILLS	SERVICE
COMPUTERS	ENTREPRENEUR	MUSIC	SPECIAL NEEDS WORKER
COOKING	FAITH	PAINTING	TEACHING
COUNSELING	GARDENING	PHOTOGRAPHY	WRITING

Day 7: A Sound Mind

Below the blank puzzle grid is a list of positive words that promote a sound mind. Place the words in the correct place on the grid. Tip: Start with letter sizes that have the fewest words. So if there are only 2 words with 7 letters and 5 words with 4 letters, try placing the 7 letter words first.

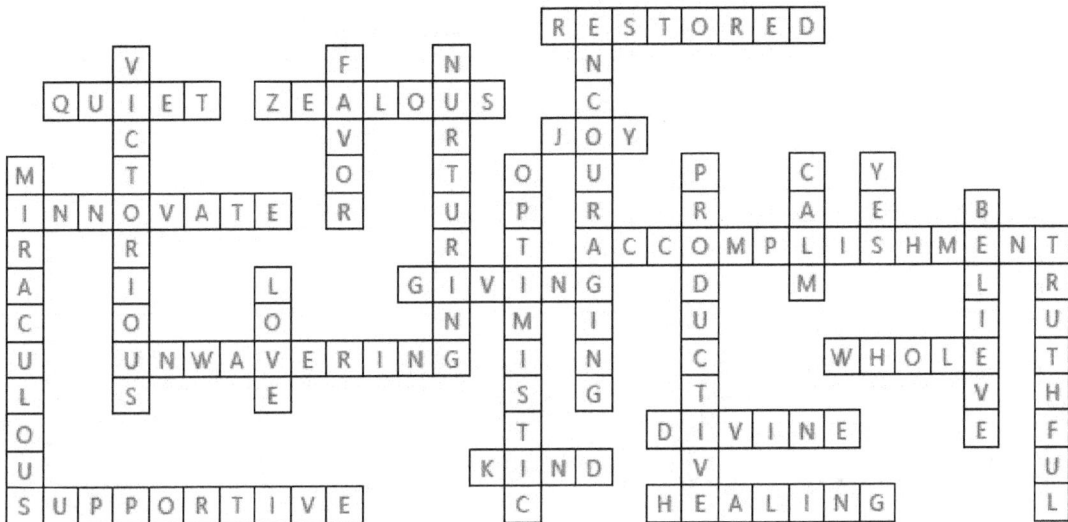

RESTORED

QUIET ZEALOUS JOY

INNOVATE ACCOMPLISHMENT

GIVING

UNWAVERING WHOLE

DIVINE

KIND

SUPPORTIVE HEALING

3 Letters	5 Letters	7 Letters	9 Letters	11 Letters
joy	favor	zealous	nurturing	encouraging
yes	whole	healing		
	quiet	believe	10 Letters	14 Letters
4 Letters			productive	accomplishment
calm	6 Letters	8 Letters	unwavering	
kind	giving	truthful	optimistic	
love	divine	restored	victorious	
		innovate	miraculous	
			supportive	

Day 8: Submission to God

The letters of the words below are jumbled. Figure out what the word is and write it on the blank line provided. Listed below are hints in the form of scriptures or definitions. All scriptures are from the New King James Version (NKJV).

1 SUSIISVBME SUBMISSIVE

2 ULER RULE

3 NEPAOTDIP APPOINTED

4 FAER FEAR

5 EIHRLTAY HEARTILY

6 LIWL WILL

7 SETT TEST

8 DEDA DEAD

9 BUITSM SUBMIT

10 OSNILWLES LOWLINESS

11 APEDYR PRAYED

12 ICDNBEOEE OBEDIENCE

13 BEULHM HUMBLE

14 UHEAOTTIIRS AUTHORITIES

15 JSECBUT SUBJECT

16 AEEPC PEACE

1. Hebrews 13:17
2. Genesis 3:16
3. Romans 13:1
4. Ephesians 5:21
5. Colossians 3:23
6. Luke 22:42
7. Jeremiah 17:10
8. Romans 7:4

9. James 4:7
10. Philippians 2:3
11. Matthew 26:39
12. Hebrews 5:8
13. 1 Peter 5:6
14. Titus 3:1
15. Romans 8:7
16. Job 22:21

Day 9: Filled with the Holy Spirit

The scripture below has been written in code. Use the hints in the decoder at the top of the page to help identify the code (the letters on top are the correct answers, the letters on the bottom are the code, one has been solved for you). Then fill-in the correct letter in the blank space above each code letter in the text. Can you find out what happens when you are filled with the Holy Spirit?

W	H	M	L	P	C	Q	S	D	Z	N	K	F	A	X	G	U	V	O	I	B	T	R	Y	J	E
A	B	C	D	E	F	G	H	I	J	K	L	M	N	O	P	Q	R	S	T	U	V	W	X	Y	Z

When the Day of Pentecost had fully
ABZK VBZ INX SM EZKVZFSHV BNI MQDDX

come they were all with one accord
FSCZ, VBZX AZWZ NDD ATVB SKZ NFFSWI

in one place   And suddenly there
TK SKZ EDNFZ.   NKI HQIIZKDX VBZWZ

came a sound from heaven as of a
FNCZ N HSQKI MWSC BZNRZK, NH SM N

rushing mighty wind and it filled
WQHBTKP CTPBVX ATKI, NKI TV MTDDZI

the whole house where they were
VBZ ABSDZ BSQHZ ABZWZ VBZX AZWZ

sitting   Then there appeared to
HTVVTKP.   VBZK VBZWZ NEEZNWZI VS

them divided tongues as of fire and
VBZC ITRTIZI VSKPQZH, NH SM MTWZ, NKI

one sat upon each of them   And they
SKZ HNV QESK ZNFB SM VBZC.   NKI VBZX

were all filled with the Holy
AZWZ NDD MTDDZI ATVB VBZ BSDX

Spirit and began to speak with other
HETWTV NKI UZPNK VS HEZNL ATVB SVBZW

tongues as the Spirit gave them
VSKPQZH, NH VBZ HETWTV PNRZ VBZC

utterance   Acts   NKJV
QVVZWNKFZ.   (NFVH 2:1-4, KLYR)

Day 10: Growth in Christ

A number of words have been removed from the scripture and placed in a word bank. Use the words from the word bank to fill in the blanks in the scripture. Write the words in the blanks provided. Challenge yourself and try to complete this without using the hint.

"Therefore, laying aside all malice, all deceit, (1) hypocrisy_____, envy, and all evil speaking, as newborn babes, desire the pure (2) milk_____ of the word, that you may (3) grow_____ thereby, if indeed you have tasted that the Lord is gracious. Coming to Him as to a living stone, rejected indeed by men, but chosen by God and precious, you also, as living stones, are being (4) built_____ (5) up_____ a spiritual house, a holy priesthood, to offer up spiritual (6) sacrifices_____ acceptable to God through Jesus Christ." (**Hint:** 1 Peter 2:1-5, NKJV)

"For this reason we also, since the day we heard it, do not cease to pray for you, and to ask that you may be filled with the (7) knowledge_____ of His will in all wisdom and spiritual (8) understanding__; that you may walk worthy of the Lord, fully pleasing Him, being (9) fruitful_____ in every good work and (10) increasing_____ in the (11) knowledge_____ of God;" (**Hint:** Colossians 1:9-10, NKJV)

"But when that which is (12) perfect_____ has come, then that which is in part will be done (13) away_____. When I was a (14) child_____, I spoke as a child, I understood as a child, I thought as a child; but when I became a man, I put away (15) childish_____ things. For now we see in a mirror, dimly, but then face to face. Now I know in (16) part_____, but then I shall know just as I also am known." (**Hint:** 1 Corinthians 13:10-12, NKJV)

up	milk	away	increasing
perfect	knowledge	part	grow
fruitful	sacrifices	hypocrisy	knowledge
built	child	understanding	childish

Day 11: Protecting Your Gates

Here are some words in which you are highly encouraged to protect your gates from. The letters of the words below are jumbled. Figure out what the word is and write it on the blank line provided. Listed below are hints in forms of definitions or descriptions.

1 TUSL LUST

2 ALCCUSUMSERI SECULARMUSIC

3 GRDEE GREED

4 HERTAD HATRED

5 CHESATINGLAEF FALSETEACHING

6 SUTERRECHPCOP CORRUPTSPEECH

7 TJERSE JESTER

8 LOTUYNTG GLUTTONY

9 REAF FEAR

10 SSPGIO GOSSIP

11 ARDMA DRAMA

12 TPIRAYFON PROFANITY

13 FTRSIE STRIFE

14 DSALERN SLANDER

15 VEYN ENVY

16 NGREA ANGER

17 RCFINOOAINT FORNICATION

18 TDALRUYE ADULTERY

1. sexual desire
2. Songs that do not glorify God
3. selfish desires
4. intense dislike or ill will
5. lies wrapped in truth
6. putrid or disgusting words to the recipient (2 words)
7. a person who habitually plays the fool
8. overeating
9. frightened or worried
10. he say, she say
11. conflicting stories or situations
12. curses
13. angry or bitter disagreement over fundamental issues
14. a false spoken statement damaging to a person's reputation
15. a feeling of discontented or resentful longing aroused by someone else's possessions
16. having a strong feeling of or showing annoyance, displeasure, or hostility
17. sex without covenant
18. infidelity

Day 12: Strengthen Your Prayer Life

In the word bank are kingdom terms that you can use in prayer. Can you find these powerful words?

```
B I N D N X L E J W I E X L L O O S E Q
C Q A G V O U K N T M X Q L N G M R T P
G J C T Z Q E I B J O O R N S W A X A Y
W L I F Q A R N Q J P A H A R C V J G Q
P R E C N I R G K B U U E F Z C I Y I F
U K P G H Q I D J P J T L C P D C B V X
A S M E I A Y O A U N H O H L O T G A K
M U S O K S J M M P B O U T H O O F N C
S S C G B J L E T M T R D U E L R C A E
Z H X A A E C A Y D O I I S E B Y N O F
R K I L R R L S T S X T V B R S K I T G
C C U F R F Z B X E M Y I O C T K F E N
S A P U T O O F G Z E J N V E R S W V S
T I R V B R J R E V E S E E D A J H G Y
M S O T C E C Z H D M U R B T U L X S
Q W O O X E M D M Y X B P R L E C N A C
K K T S I S J E E Z O C D U Y G P G I B
L G Z M W R O R B E G W Q L E I F M X U
I A L O C J S Q X Y M N G E Z E R N I L
I V L S G M B G M Y I D M T A S U B F I
```

AUTHORITY	BIND	BLOOD	CANCEL
COSMOS	DECREE	DIVINE	FORCES
KINGDOM	LEGISLATE	LOOSE	NAVIGATE
OVERRULE	REDEEM	SEVER	SHIFT

The Daniel Way: 21 Days of Fasting and Prayer to Reboot Your Entire Being

Day 13: Greater Wisdom

A number of words have been removed from the scripture and placed in a word bank. Use the words from the word bank to fill in the blanks in the scripture. Write the words in the blanks provided. Challenge yourself and try to complete this without using the hint. (Hint: Colossians 2:2-32, NKJV)

"that their (1) hearts may be (2) encouraged, being knit together in

(3) love, and (4) attaining to all (5) riches of the full

assurance of (6) understanding, to the knowledge of the (7) mystery of

God, both of the (8) Father and of (9) Christ, in whom are

(10) hidden all the treasures of (11) wisdom and

(12) knowledge . "

Christ	mystery	understanding	knowledge	encouraged
love	hidden	attaining	Father	hearts
riches	wisdom			

Day 14: Being a Faithful Steward

Here are some words that pertains to being a faithful steward. The letters of the words below are jumbled. Figure out what the word is and write it on the blank line provided. Listed below are hints in the form of definitions or descriptions.

1 EUSLUF USEFUL

2 TOTNIECMMM COMMITMENT

3 TUFILAFH FAITHFUL

4 NVSATER SERVANT

5 DEADECDIT DEDICATED

6 EDELRA LEADER

7 ANCLGLI CALLING

8 PELRNSSOIBE RESPONSIBLE

9 ENSLATT TALENTS

10 IFSGT GIFTS

11 EVIG GIVE

12 NAGEAM MANAGE

1. able to be used for a practical purpose or in several ways

2. an engagement or obligation that restricts freedom of action

3. royal, constant, and steadfast

4. a person who performs duties for others

5. devoted to a task or purpose

6. the person who leads or commands a group, organization, or country.

7. a strong inner impulse toward a particular course of action

8. having an obligation to do something, or having control over or care for someone

9. a special often athletic, creative, or artistic aptitude

10. a natural ability or talent

11. provide or supply with.

12. be in charge of

Day 15: The Fruit of the Spirit

Provide the word that best matches each clue.

1 LONGSUFFERING (PATIENCE)   Self-restraint before proceeding to action

2 TEMPERANCE (SELF-CONTROL)   Continence

3 GENTLENESS   usefulness, excellence (in character or demeanor)

4 FAITH   Firm persuasion, to win over, conviction in the truth

5 PEACE   wholeness, soundness, health, well-being, prosperity

6 MEEKNESS   Gentleness by implying humility

7 GOODNESS   Active goodness

8 LOVE   to have affectionate regard

9 JOY   gladness

goodness	joy	peace
meekness	faith	love
gentleness	longsuffering (patience)	temperance (self-control)

Day 16: Obedience

Answer the questions to the devotional you just read by providing the letter of the word which best answers the question.

1 _A_ Obedience is an act of what?
  A. LOVE B. MANKIND C. HUMILITY D. TO HEAR OR LISTEN

2 _D_ What is better than sacrifice?
  A. MANKIND B. HUMILITY C. TO LISTEN TO D. OBEY

3 _C_ How should Christians position themselves?
  A. MANKIND B. JESUS C. HUMILITY D. LOVE

4 _A_ What does the Greek word "hupotasso" mean?
  A. TO RANK UNDER B. TO HEAR OR LISTEN C. HUMILITY D. LOVE

5 _D_ Who is the greatest example of obedience
  A. OBEY B. LOVE C. HUMILITY D. JESUS

6 _B_ Who or what obeyed God first?
  A. TO RANK UNDER B. ANIMALS C. HUMILITY D. OBEDIENCE

7 _C_ What does the Hebrew word "shema" means?
  A. LOVE B. ANIMALS C. TO HEAR OR LISTEN D. OBEDIENCE

8 _C_ Worship is a form of what?
  A. MANKIND B. HUMILITY C. OBEDIENCE D. JESUS

9 _C_ Which creation has a tendency to disobey God?
  A. OBEDIENCE B. HUMILITY C. MANKIND D. OBEY

10 _B_ What does the Greek word "hupakouo" mean?
  A. MANKIND B. TO LISTEN TO C. ANIMALS D. OBEDIENCE

Day 17: Communication

Listed below are some tips for effective communication. Read the prompt and decide if it is concerning listening or hearing.

1 _B_ Don't rush or cut the other person off.
A. LISTENING   B. SPOKEN

2 _B_ Try to block out distractions.
A. SPOKEN   B. LISTENING

3 _A_ Ask questions to show you are interested and to clarify things you aren't sure of.
A. LISTENING   B. SPOKEN

4 _A_ Don't talk just to fill the silence.
A. SPOKEN   B. LISTENING

5 _B_ Don't focus on rehearsing what you will say next.
A. SPOKEN   B. LISTENING

6 _A_ If the person expresses strong feelings, try to acknowledge them without becoming offended or angry yourself.
A. LISTENING   B. SPOKEN

7 _A_ Be respectful.
A. SPOKEN   B. LISTENING

8 _A_ Be forgiving.
A. SPOKEN   B. LISTENING

9 _B_ Speak clearly, avoiding jargon and confusing ramblings.
A. LISTENING   B. SPOKEN

10 _B_ Smile and look the other person in the eye naturally
A. SPOKEN   B. LISTENING

11 _A_ Look for common ground.
A. LISTENING   B. SPOKEN

12 _B_ Express appreciation and encouragement
A. LISTENING   B. SPOKEN

13 _A_ Apologize when needed
A. SPOKEN   B. LISTENING

14 _B_ Use "I" statements instead of accusing.
A. LISTENING   B. SPOKEN

Day 18: Believers Prayer

Here is a list of people who you can pray for. Pray for them as you mark them off.

```
Z G S K C A T T A T S I R O R R E T C M
S R E D N O P S E R T S R I F T S P Z F
L W R Q G B D F G W D A D N S D C N V W
P S T U C O T U O F R L U N U K U E C F
R T K G C B E Z V S U P R E A C H E R S
H V Y T E C A E E W G N D W I V E S P R
X C O W G L C I R B A E M F M N L S M G
Z R K N M J H C N O D R U Q A M Y R P E
S Q C H P Y E J M F D D S W B F Z E F K
J U W N H E R W E J I L R F R Q D R K U
M C D M A W S T N L C I M E L O K E Y N
N A M E R I F E T A T H F T P K X D F O
G Y T T M X C V Q W S C P H M K K R Q O
O S P S A O I F T Y G X I S E G D U J K
S Y Z A C Q Q H H E M L C D W T J M F J
T B D X I R A Z I R E Z P N D R I W J N
O R V J S Z P I H S R E D A E L D V Z Z
L F D X T N K S Z G N H U S B A N D S F
I H B V S P X L Q T E E N A G E R S A K
P D M T N E M E C R O F N E W A L P Y Q
```

CHILDREN | JUDGES | PILOTS
DOCTORS | LAW ENFORCEMENT | PREACHERS
DRUG ADDICTS | LAWYERS | TEACHERS
FIREMAN | LEADERSHIP | TEENAGERS
FIRST RESPONDERS | MURDERERS | TERRORIST ATTACKS
GOVERNMENT | PEDOPHILES | WIVES
HUSBANDS | PHARMACISTS

The Daniel Way: 21 Days of Fasting and Prayer to Reboot Your Entire Being

Day 19: Relationships

Below the blank puzzle grid is a list of positive words that promotes healthy relationships. Place the words in the correct place on the grid. Tip: Start with letter sizes that have the fewest words. So if there are only 2 words with 7 letters and 5 words with 4 letters, try placing the 7 letter words first.

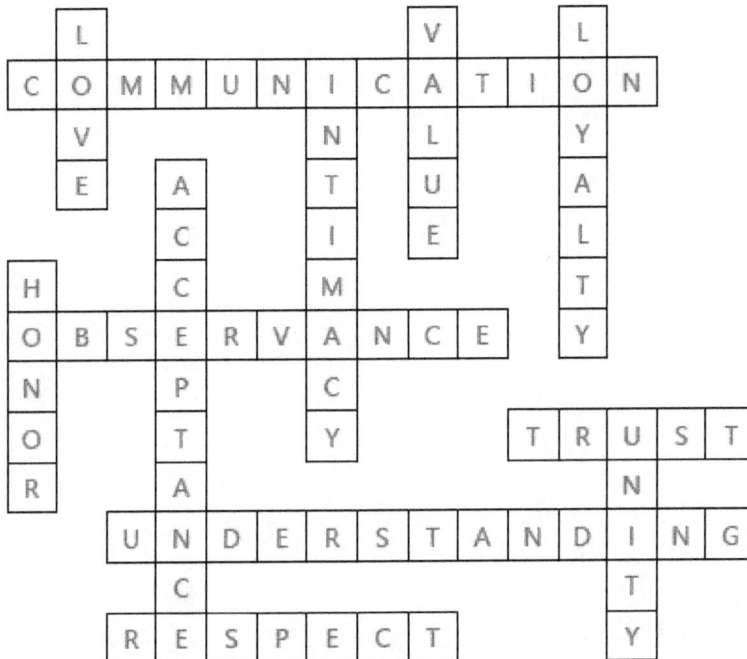

4 Letters	TRUST	8 Letters	13 Letters
LOVE		INTIMACY	UNDERSTANDING
	7 Letters		COMMUNICATION
5 Letters	RESPECT	10 Letters	
HONOR	LOYALTY	OBSERVANCE	
VALUE		ACCEPTANCE	
UNITY			

The Daniel Way: 21 Days of Fasting and Prayer to Reboot Your Entire Being

Day 20: Expectation

Find the hidden words that are associated with expectation.

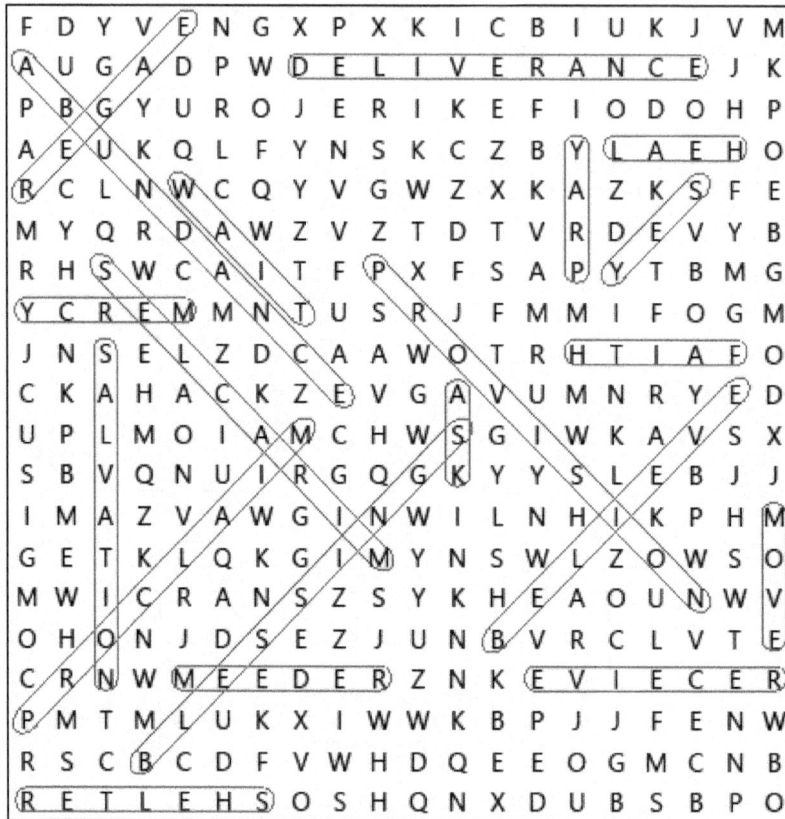

```
F  D  Y  V  E  N  G  X  P  X  K  I  C  B  I  U  K  J  V  M
A  U  G  A  D  P  W  D  E  L  I  V  E  R  A  N  C  E  J  K
P  B  G  Y  U  R  O  J  E  R  I  K  E  F  I  O  D  O  H  P
A  E  U  K  Q  L  F  Y  N  S  K  C  Z  B  Y  L  A  E  H  O
R  C  L  N  W  C  Q  Y  V  G  W  Z  X  K  A  Z  K  S  F  E
M  Y  Q  R  D  A  W  Z  V  Z  T  D  T  V  R  D  E  V  Y  B
R  H  S  W  C  A  I  T  F  P  X  F  S  A  P  Y  T  B  M  G
Y  C  R  E  M  M  N  T  U  S  R  J  F  M  M  I  F  O  G  M
J  N  S  E  L  Z  D  C  A  A  W  O  T  R  H  T  I  A  F  O
C  K  A  H  A  C  K  Z  E  V  G  A  V  U  M  N  R  Y  E  D
U  P  L  M  O  I  A  M  C  H  W  S  G  I  W  K  A  V  S  X
S  B  V  Q  N  U  I  R  G  Q  G  K  Y  Y  S  L  E  B  J  J
I  M  A  Z  V  A  W  G  I  N  W  I  L  N  H  I  K  P  H  M
G  E  T  K  L  Q  K  G  I  M  Y  N  S  W  L  Z  O  W  S  O
M  W  I  C  R  A  N  S  Z  S  Y  K  H  E  A  O  U  N  W  V
O  H  O  N  J  D  S  E  Z  J  U  N  B  V  R  C  L  V  T  E
C  R  N  W  M  E  E  D  E  R  Z  N  K  E  V  I  E  C  E  R
P  M  T  M  L  U  K  X  I  W  W  K  B  P  J  J  F  E  N  W
R  S  C  B  C  D  F  V  W  H  D  Q  E  E  O  G  M  C  N  B
R  E  T  L  E  H  S  O  S  H  Q  N  X  D  U  B  S  B  P  O
```

ABUNDANCE	EAGER	MOVE	REDEEM
ASK	FAITH	PRAY	SALVATION
BELIEVE	HEAL	PROCLAIM	SHELTER
BLESSINGS	MERCY	PROVISION	WAIT
DELIVERANCE	MIRACLES	RECEIVE	YES

The Daniel Way: 21 Days of Fasting and Prayer to Reboot Your Entire Being

Day 21: Release

Find the hidden words that are associated with release.

```
P  H  I  Q  B  L  P  J  F  S  C  A  K  R  X  X  E  G  I  G
O  Y  R  H  V  E  K  Z  K  U  O  D  F  N  W  U  N  Z  S  U
B  C  E  A  G  X  X  Q  A  T  U  C  Z  D  C  O  W  I  G  B
M  N  C  C  J  O  H  P  M  E  H  M  Y  S  I  Q  A  Q  Q  A
G  E  N  A  E  N  G  B  R  X  G  W  E  T  W  Z  L  L  Y  P
N  M  A  Y  N  E  S  L  W  C  O  R  U  M  Q  C  K  E  T  P
J  E  T  G  N  R  O  C  E  Q  H  L  A  A  Z  M  O  U  I  D
X  L  T  T  C  A  Q  N  J  M  O  F  Q  H  C  Y  U  R  N  E
B  C  I  N  T  T  R  T  O  S  A  M  U  N  C  B  T  N  U  L
Q  Y  U  A  Q  I  R  A  B  I  K  N  J  H  U  S  J  E  M  I
P  N  Q  M  T  O  V  A  N  L  T  S  C  T  L  A  I  F  M  V
H  Z  C  Z  F  N  X  I  I  S  T  A  T  I  M  V  P  D  L  E
M  V  A  T  Z  M  V  B  V  W  O  C  G  N  P  L  F  Z  X  R
W  O  T  T  C  N  E  N  B  A  X  M  E  R  U  A  A  C  W  A
G  R  D  Z  V  R  T  O  I  R  Q  S  M  E  U  O  T  L  Q  N
B  Q  X  E  A  Y  Q  D  I  G  T  G  K  D  G  P  M  I  U  C
V  R  L  T  E  S  X  R  V  Y  F  E  I  L  E  R  M  U  O  E
Q  D  I  G  R  E  A  W  B  I  C  O  I  K  R  E  O  I  N
M  O  L  K  A  D  F  P  E  X  E  M  P  T  I  O  N  Z  C  D
N  R  W  P  V  B  N  S  S  P  R  I  N  G  I  Y  N  Z  Y  O
```

ABSOLUTION	DISCHARGE	PARDON
ACQUITTANCE	EMANCIPATION	RANSOM
AMNESTY	EXEMPTION	RELIEF
BAIL	EXONERATION	RESCUE
CLEMENCY	FREEDOM	SPRING
COMPURGATION	IMMUNITY	WALKOUT

The Daniel Way: 21 Days of Fasting and Prayer to Reboot Your Entire Being

To view more titles from the author, visit

TRAINING GROUND
PUBLICATIONS

www.TrainingGroundPublications.com

www.ingramcontent.com/pod-product-compliance
Lightning Source LLC
LaVergne TN
LVHW081352060426
835510LV00013B/1786